© Eileen Barroso / Columbia University

JOHN MCWHORTER is an associate professor of English and comparative literature at Columbia University and is the author of sixteen books, including *The Language Hoax*, *The Power of Babel*, and *Our Magnificent Bastard Tongue*. He writes for *Time*, CNN, *The Wall Street Journal*, and *The Atlantic*, and his articles have also appeared in *The New York Times*, *The New Yorker*, *Los Angeles Times*, *The Washington Post*, *New Republic*, and *The Daily Beast*.

ALSO BY JOHN McWHORTER

The Language Hoax: Why the World Looks the Same in Any Language

What Language Is: And What It Isn't and What It Could Be

Linguistic Simplicity and Complexity: Why Do Languages Undress?

Our Magnificent Bastard Tongue: The Untold History of English

All About the Beat: Why Hip-Hop Can't Save Black America

Language Interrupted: Signs of Non-Native Acquisition in Standard Language Grammars

Winning the Race: Beyond the Crisis in Black America

Defining Creole

Doing Our Own Thing: The Degradation of Language and Music and Why We Should, Like, Care

Authentically Black: Essays for the Black Silent Majority

The Power of Babel: A Natural History of Language

Losing the Race: Self-Sabotage in Black America

Spreading the Word: Language and Dialect in America

Word on the Street: Debunking the Myth of a "Pure" Standard English

The Missing Spanish Creoles: Recovering the Birth of Plantation Contact Languages

Towards a New Model of Creole Genesis

Words on the Move

Why English Won't—
and Can't—Sit Still
(Like, Literally)

WORDS

on the

MOVE

John McWhorter

Picador   Henry Holt and Company   New York

picadorusa.com • picadorbookroom.tumblr.com
twitter.com/picadorusa • facebook.com/picadorusa

Picador® is a U.S. registered trademark and is used by Macmillan Publishing Group, LLC, under license from Pan Books Limited.

For book club information, please visit facebook.com/picadorbookclub or email marketing@picadorusa.com.

Designed by Kelly S. Too

The Library of Congress has cataloged the Henry Holt edition as follows:

Names: McWhorter, John H., author.
Title: Words on the move : why English wont and cant sit still (like, literally) / John McWhorter.
Description: New York : Henry Holt and Co., 2016. | Includes index.
Identifiers: LCCN 2015050775 | ISBN 9781627794718 (hardcover) | ISBN 9781627794732 (ebook)
Subjects: LCSH: Linguistic change. | Language and languages—Variation. | Language and languages—Etymology. | Sociolinguistics. | BISAC: LANGUAGE ARTS & DISCIPLINES / Linguistics / Etymology. | LANGUAGE ARTS & DISCIPLINES / Grammar & Punctuation.
Classification: LCC P40.5.L54 M39 2015 | DDC 417'.7—dc23
LC record available at http://lccn.loc.gov/2015050775

Picador Paperback ISBN 978-1-250-14378-5

Our books may be purchased in bulk for promotional, educational, or business use. Please contact your local bookseller or the Macmillan Corporate and Premium Sales Department at 1-800-221-7945, extension 5442, or by email at MacmillanSpecialMarkets@macmillan.com.

First published by Henry Holt & Company, LLC

First Picador Edition: September 2017

D 10 19 8 7 6 5

To Martha.

I said having children would mean I would stop writing these.
You didn't want me to, I couldn't, and thank you for enabling
(in both senses) my habit.

Contents

Contents

Words on the Move

Introduction

No one minds that today the clouds are neither in the same position nor in the same shapes they were yesterday. Yet more than a few mind that today the way people are talking is always changing.

Of course, if polled, few of us would put a check next to the statement "I think language should never change." However, so often we don't like it when the change actually happens. Somehow it seems that language is always changing in the *wrong ways*.

It would seem that when most people express approval of language changing, they are thinking of something relatively nondisruptive: roughly, matters of keeping the language up to date. Certainly we will always need new words for new things. Historical transformations, especially, will change the language—it seems natural that our English is vastly different from the English of people seven hundred years ago living under a feudalist monarchy without electricity, photography, jazz, or penicillin. And most of us are okay with some slang coming and going—although, even here, many would seem to prefer that it be only so much.

Beyond that, things get touchy. When it comes to people using *literally* to mean what would seem to be its opposite, "figuratively" (*I was itching so much I was literally about to die!*), or *like* with a frequency that makes it sound more like punctuation than a word, the linguist may preach to the public that our language is dynamic, but to many, the better word would be degraded.

When Samuel Johnson started assembling what would become the first true dictionary of the English language, in the mid-eighteenth century, he felt the same way about the changes in speech he had heard throughout his life. At first he hoped that his opus would help stop this messiness once and for all, by enshrining the language in the frozen state of print. Yet by the time he finished the project, he had come to realize that this was an impossible task:

> We laugh at the elixir that promises to prolong life to a thousand years; and with equal justice may the lexicographer be derided, who being able to produce no example of a nation that has preserved their words and phrases from mutability; shall imagine that his dictionary can embalm his language, and secure it from corruption and decay.

Johnson surely sounds wise, ahead of the curve. Yet a modern English speaker may easily receive Johnson's opinion as wisdom while at the same time gnashing his teeth over people using *literally* "the wrong way." After all, Johnson lived a very long time ago; one may feel on a certain level that when it comes to language as we live and breathe it today, things are different.

But they aren't. One of hardest notions for a human being to shake is that a language is something that *is*, when it is actually something always *becoming*. They tell you a word is a thing, when it's actually something going on.

Yet, in real time, a word's going on often feels more like it's going off—as in off the rails. Rather marvelous, then, is that precisely the kinds of things that sound so disorderly, so inattendant, so "wrong," are precisely how Latin became French. The way people under a certain age use *totally* and the pronunciation of *nuclear* as "nucular" are not some alternate kind of language change sitting alongside the "real" kind. Language change like this is all there has ever been.

It isn't that language changes only because new things need names or because new developments bring people into new contacts. Language changes because its very structure makes transformation inevitable. To wit: even if a language were spoken by a community mysteriously condemned to live for millennia in a cave, under staunchly unchanging conditions, after three thousand years the language of that community would be vastly different from the one spoken when they were first herded into the cave, and outsiders would most likely hear it as a different language entirely. In Old English, for example, the word pronounced GAHST-litch meant "spiritual," but as sounds shuffled around or wore away and its very meaning drifted along, it became our modern English word *ghostly*—imagine that kind of thing happening to thousands of words bit by bit. Yet, obviously, little of what we could call "dynamic" would have happened in the cave. The change would happen simply because mutability is as inherent to the very nature of language as it is for clouds to be ever in transformation.

With clouds, change comes as the consequence of wind currents, temperature, and barometric pressure, things structurally eternal. In a similar way, permanent aspects of human anatomy and cognition are why language is as changeable as clouds are. Buzzing quietly around a word's main meaning are assorted submeanings and implications, which have a way of creeping into how we actually use the word until its very meaning is forever transformed: hence a word meaning "spiritual" comes to refer to a particular kind of spirit, ghosts.

We should, for instance, be able to say that we find *2001: A Space Odyssey* and *Citizen Kane* adorable. After all, so many people do adore those films. Yet there is a certain quiet kick in applying the vastness of "adoration" to something small, such as a child, or to someone perceived as small in an extended sense. To grant "adoration" to the small feels generous and thus sincere. Enough people savored that good feeling that after a while, *adorable* meant something more specific than admired: it came to mean "charming," pleasing in a way associated with that which is little, immature, inferior, or dear to us. (The intersection between those four traits is, in itself, vaguely alarming!) Curious George is adorable; the Statue of Liberty, not so much.

Meanwhile, sounds are slightly misheard by each generation's ears, with each generation making the sounds slightly differently. A word many once pronounced "dafter" now is only pronounced "dawter"; hence our familiar *daughter*. (There's a reason it's spelled like *laughter*!) This is much of why the actors in old movies sound increasingly odd to us as the decades pass. It's not only that they are making references to Calvin Coolidge and calling things "swell," but that our very "accent" has morphed on from theirs.

Processes like this are exactly what creates the language we speak as opposed to the way dead people did. Yet we tend to have an easier time with weather than with language change. Much of the reason for that is something as majestic in itself as dictionaries.

Samuel Johnson's gift to the language was also, in an unintended way, a curse upon its speakers. We are accustomed to writers opening an exploration of a concept by citing a word's definition in the dictionary, with the implication that words have eternal meanings just as numbers have values and atoms have certain combinations of subatomic particles. Dictionaries are large; the densely printed pages packed with information are fine music to any book person; dictionaries also tend to smell good. One loves them. Yet the weird truth is that for all their artifactual splendor, dictionaries are starkly misleading portraits of something as endlessly transforming as language. In terms of how words actually exist in time and space, to think of a word's "genuine" meaning as the one you find upon looking it up is like designating a middle-aged person's high school graduation snapshot as "what they really look like." There's a charming whimsy in it, but still. A person receiving such a compliment often says, "Oh, please!"—and words, if they could talk, surely would as well.

But words can't talk. Meanwhile, dictionaries are there, in all their weight, permanence—fragrance, even. The ancient brown ones look especially eternal, granitic, like the old library buildings they are often found in. Surely, here is where a language resides. Naturally, departures from the dictionary come off as decay and chaos. Maybe new words for new things are okay—but even there, many have a hard time with lexicographers deeming *vape* and *Not!* as "real words," no matter how common they are in our experience.

But there's a lot you can miss in a dictionary. If you can't create *vape* from *vapor*, then why do dictionaries have *peddle* when the word didn't exist until people made it up from the word *pedlar*? Why does *Darn!* make it in when it came from a quiet mashup of the *damn* in *damnation* and the *-tern-* part of *eternal* when people were given to saying *Eternal damnation!* a lot? (That *Tarnation!* expression we associate with old gold prospectors was a middle step in the process.) We are unlikely to catch those things amid the massiveness of the dictionary, and besides, *peddle* and *Darn!* are, well, "olde." *Vape* and *Not!* are just . . . different? It's hard not to think so: life is slow, dictionaries are big, and novelty is unsettling.

But novelty can also be a lot of fun. Some consider it the staff of life. It's certainly what keeps most linguists so interested in language—but we don't share it enough. In this book I want to help change that.

It must be clear that this will not be one more book about a certain collection of what we might call "blackboard grammar" rules. Largely, that debate has come to a prickly stalemate, and no new arguments will likely make much difference. Many of these rules, such as the idea that one is to say *It is I*, and not split an infinitive or end a sentence with a preposition, are more discussed than actually observed today. For most of the others, such as that one is to say *Billy and I went to the store* rather than *Billy and me*, that one is neither to entirely dismiss *whom* nor to use double negatives, that there are fewer, not less, books, and that one is to say *Go slowly* rather than *Go slow*, the verdict is essentially in. Linguists endlessly remind us that these rules are arbitrary, unconnected to clarity or logic. Yet no linguist denies the other reality, which is that these rules, having been entrenched in society as measures of formality and social worth, must be followed in formal contexts and taught to young people. It is inevitable for humans to rank, to create hierarchies of estimation, often on the basis of differences unparseable by logic: the proper analogy is with fashions in clothing.*

In the wake of conclusive discussions of these grammar rules, such as many of David Crystal's publications and, most recently, Steven Pinker's book *The Sense of Style*, there is little need to dwell on them further. This book will focus on something larger, in a way, than that compact collection of grammatical no-nos: the general sense that when English is morphing along in any way (new accents, new meanings) we are seeing not transformation but disruption. I want to

---

* One rule seems especially resistant to détente: the idea is that one is not to use *they* in the plural as in *Tell each student they can hand in their paper tomorrow*. However, I suspect that with changing perceptions and courtesies regarding gender identity in our times, measured usage of the singular *they* will occasion ever less condemnation even in formal contexts.

propose a sunny (and, frankly, scientifically accurate) way
of hearing the speech around us, as a substitute for a view
of English as a collection of words embalmed between the
covers of dictionaries.

In a way, I want to take you backward. It was not until the
eighteenth century, as the middle class in England and
the United States became numerous and powerful enough
to develop a focused self-consciousness about their self-
presentation as members of said class, that this glum, con-
demnatory sense of the language around us truly settled in.
The acrid views expressed about colloquial speech in online
comments sections today is a relatively *new* view of language, fostered by a combination of bourgeois sensibility
and the dominance of unchanging documents such as
dictionaries, both of which subtly but powerfully distract
us from the dynamic reality of language's essential mech-
anisms.

Indeed, the way we are taught to process language is as
antique as our ancestors' sense of how nature worked. The
first generations of people living under today's conception
of English in the late eighteenth and early nineteenth
century were also taught that all the world's animals were
created at one time, unaware that animals are the product of
endless evolution over vast periods. When Charles Darwin
presented the latter proposition, people were at first deeply
skeptical—but consensus moved on. To carry the analogy
further, just as many today are most comfortable with the
idea of language changing in response to large-scale historical events, there were those who subscribed to the natural-
ist Georges Cuvier's idea that fossils of now-extinct animals

showed that animals had been created anew after each of a series of global "catastrophes." But, in retrospect, even that concession is all but unrecognizable to us today as science.

And just as we cherish science because it teaches us new things rather than just describing what we already know, under a scientific view of what the language around us is like, so very much makes sense instead of seeming merely curious. *Why* is Shakespearean language harder for us to understand in performance than it was for people five hundred years ago? *Why* do younger people sound like they talk in questions, with their pitch rising uuP at the end of their sentences? *Why* do civilized euphemisms such as *disabled* so often get reclassified as quaint or even insulting? *Why* does that woman you know pronounce her boss Nick's name more like "Neck"? *Why* is it so hard to truly accept that there is a "dialect" called Black English? *Why* does William Powell in *The Thin Man* say that he is going to round up all the sus-PECTS instead of the SUS-pects? (I'm sure you've always wondered about that!) *Why* have emoticons caught on to such a degree? *Why* do women say "um" more while men say "uh" more? (Actually, on that one nobody knows!)

This book will answer all those questions (or, in the case of the last one, refer to it) and many more. The answers require understanding a mere five ways that language changes. The question is not *whether* a word will undergo one or more of these processes, but which ones of them it *will* go through. We do not watch a parade and wonder why those people don't just *stand still*. Language is a parade: the word whose sound and meaning stays the same over centuries is the exception rather than the rule. If that kind of change is precisely why we speak Modern English rather than the language of Chaucer and don't mind a bit, then today's changes ought to inspire curiosity rather than perplexity: "Where's the language going next?" rather than "What's *that* all about?"

This book will show us what it's about, getting us past the perceptual detour English speakers have been shunted into over the past few centuries, and back to the way earlier generations saw the fluidity of language around them. Let us go, as it were, back to the future.

1

The Faces of English

Words Get Personal

There's a reason that it often requires an art history class to get a handle on medieval painting. It may be pretty in a general sense, but it's hard not to notice that the people tend to exhibit only the broadest of emotions, if any—in much of medieval painting, the faces seem almost frozen blank.

It would never have occurred to a painter like Giotto to depict the full range of human expressions. The individualist focus that seems so natural to us was not yet a part of how one was taught to create art. Art was less about you, him, or her than about *that*: grander things such as religion and commemoration. We cherish the *Mona Lisa* as one of the heralds of the new era, with that smile we can imagine someone curling into near the middle of a good first date. And even that doesn't compare with the japingly sarcastic glow on the face of the Cossack scribe penning an insulting letter to the Turkish sultan in Elias Repin's most famous painting, *Zaporozhian Cossacks of Ukraine Writing a Mocking Letter to the Turkish Sultan,* of 1891. It's lifelike in a fashion we'd never find in a Byzantine image.

This increasing focus on the individual is a theme in much of Western history. We can practically hear and smell Anna Karenina, Holden Caulfield, and Oscar Wao in a way that we never can any of the characters in *The Iliad.* To Plato and Aristotle, steeped in unquestioningly hierarchical ideologies, a political system guaranteeing all individuals "life, liberty and the pursuit of happiness" would have sounded like science fiction. Even the notion of a popular song "cover" is a sign of the times. To Cole Porter, it would have seemed alien to write a song for only one artist to sing, with anyone else required to wait about ten years to take a crack at it, and even then, have their effort classified as a salutary "version" of the first one. Today, a pop song is about one person expressing their one self.

Language, however, has always been ahead of the curve on individualism. Long before Rembrandt, Thomas Jefferson, or Adele, human language has always and forever been getting personal. Not in the sense of people having arguments, although of course that has been happening, too. Rather, one of the things that has always happened to a great many words is that they start out showing what we *mean,* but end up being used to show how we *feel.* This trajectory is as common as words getting shorter (*I'd-a done it* from *I would have done it*), cuter (*horsey, brewsky*), or nastier (*hussy* started as *housewife*). Just as often, a word nestles into a place in English that grammar mavens and quite a few others consider unsuitably vague, random, redundant, or as having no "real" meaning—the use of *so* at the start of a sentence is an example—when to a linguist the word in question is fulfilling a function as normal as marking past tense or making something plural.

This chapter will introduce you to something very old about language that, through no fault of our own, always seems new.

Well, What?

It's a whole wing of language that one hears too little about, with our natural intuition that a word is something with a meaning corresponding to some easily specified thing, concept, action, or quality. Ah, there is so much more to what it is to communicate as a human being. There are certainly the vanilla sentences. *Horses run fast*: if a toddler asks us what that means, we could easily go word by word and nail the matter. But then, how about another perfectly plausible sentence: *Well, horses run fast*. Okay: *horses*, *run*, and *fast* are easy. But what about *well*? What does *well* mean, Mommy? Note, this is not the *well* that refers to excellence: you didn't mean *Expertly, horses run fast*. This is that other little *well*, that you don't even think about.

Why did you say *well*, Mommy? Tough, isn't it? If we must, you use *well* that way to politely acknowledge a previous statement, usually before expressing some view counter to it. That is, you would say *Well, horses run fast* if someone had asked, out of genuine curiosity, why horses don't seem to get eaten by wolves. The *well* would nod politely to the person's ignorance on the topic before affording them the knowledge that horses run too fast to be caught by canines. With *well* you convey, of all things, a gracious attitude. To speak English is to know that subconsciously.

And when it's that hard to specify or master what a particular word "means," it's a good sign that we're in a different realm of language, where the tidy idea of nouns, verbs, adverbs, and conjunctions you learned in school doesn't do much for you, and a *Schoolhouse Rock!* jingle would be frustratingly diagonal. "Conjunction Junction" and "A Noun Is a Person, Place, or Thing!" were delightfully instructive tunes, but it's hard to imagine setting a melody to "*Well* implies discrepancy between a previous statement and what you wish to utter!" or at least one that would exactly catch on.

Why it would be hard to write a jingle about *well* is that it's about not labeling and describing, but something more abstract and subjective: attitude. *Well* allows us to indicate our take on what we're talking about; in this case, wanting to amend what someone has just said but without causing offense. *Horse* is objective; *well* is subjective. *Horse* is what you call something; *well* is about why you want to bring the horse up at all. *Well* is personal, and it is hardly alone: it is part of an aspect of language as central to being a person as naming things and saying what they do.

What is this realm of language called? I have held off because the term is one that seems almost designed to confuse. A more familiar concept is *semantics*: this refers to what words "mean" in the conventional sense. A horse is that magnificently peculiar animal; running is locomotion at a quick pace. However, when the issue is words used to indicate our attitude toward what we are saying, the topic is *pragmatics*. Ugh. We think of *pragmatic* as meaning "practical," but if anything, it's steak-and-potatoes semantics that seems practical compared to the subjectivity of a word like *well* in *Well, horses run fast*.

Linguists adopted the term *pragmatism* through its already abstractified usage by philosophers, referring to a school treating thought as not just mirroring reality in a passive way, but affording and mediating engagement with a surrounding environment in a more proactive, *pragmatic* way. Note the analogy between semantics, which is merely about naming and defining, and this other realm of language, which is about mediating emotionally between us and that which has been defined—in a practical, or *pragmatic*, fashion along the lines of the philosophical usage.

However, pragmatics is actually too broad a term for what I want to open up for you in this chapter. Getting our feelings in is only one part of what pragmatics entails. Pragmatics is also about what we want to call attention to (No, *that* sock, not this one!), what we want to leave in the background in order to get on to a new topic (*Anyway*, it's over now and we need to start on the new one), initiating a new topic without seeming abrupt (*So*, I heard there's a new way to peel garlic), and other things. Our concern is the personal, subjective wing of pragmatics, for which one term is *modal*, as in mood. In a sentence like *Well, horses run fast*, a word like *well* lends a note of personal orientation that often seems out of place in print statements, with a meaning so abstract that one almost wants to say it isn't a "real word." Our concern, then, is what linguists call modal pragmatic markers: we shall term them MPMs, but soon we'll exchange that term for something more user-friendly. For now, the point is less the jargon than that having MPMs and generating new MPMs is a normal process in any language.

Any language is always dragging some words from the chipper, gingham-dress, schoolroom straightforwardness of semantics (Horses live on farms!) into the MPM maw: layered, loaded, smoking Dunhills in the courtyard. MPMs are evidence of a word that started as an ordinary one, but then got personal.

The Personal Pull

MPMs are an extreme manifestation of a general process. Throughout any language, words of all kinds are always going personal to a certain extent: the subjective exerts a gravity-style pull on words' meanings. Example: *must* started out in the objective command sense: *You must stand still.* Later came an alternate meaning of *must*, as in (doorbell rings) *That must be the Indian food.* In saying that, we don't mean "I demand that that be the Indian food," but a more personal, subjective sense of mustness. You mean that within your mind and your sense of what is likely, logic requires that you *must* suppose that it's the Indian food, rather than the mail or a neighbor. First was the command meaning, objective and focused outward. But over time words often turn inward and become more about you. "That" (in my mind) "must be the Indian food": here is psychology. *Must* got personal.

Other times, things get so personal that the original meaning vanishes entirely. Here's some Tennyson (sorry): Lancelot's admirer Elaine is asleep "Till rathe she rose, half-cheated in the thought." Rathe? Angry, as in "wrathed," maybe? No, actually: the word meant "quick" or, in this passage, "early." Elaine is up early with things on her mind. *Rathe* meant "early," so *rath-er*, in Old and into Middle English, meant "earlier." But a meaning like that was ripe for going personal, as *must* did. It happens via what we could call *meaning creep*, by analogy with the term *mission creep*—bit by bit, new shades creep into what we consider the meaning of something to be, until one day the meaning has moved so far from the original one that it seems almost astounding.

What happened with *rather* is that something you've got going earlier or sooner is often something you like better. As such, if *rather* means "earlier," then there's an air about *rather* not only of sunrise, but of preferability. That is, to earlier English speakers, *rather* was as much about what you like better (something personal) as about the more concrete issue of what you do before you do something else. Today the relationship between the two meanings is clearer in *sooner*. In saying, "I'd sooner die than marry him," you mean not that you'd prefer your death to precede your nuptials, but that you don't want to marry the man in question. Over time, meaning creep of this kind can leave the original meaning in the dust, which is what happened with *rather*. *Rather* got so personal that its original meaning is now an archaism of the kind that throws us in reading Tennyson.

MPMs are what happens when this personal pull on words' meanings goes so far that a word no longer has what we can easily process as a meaning at all (*Well*, . . .), or has a meaning so divorced from the original that some mistake seems to have been made (the "teenager" usage of *like*).

In these cases, the word's very essence has become an expression of personal feeling, rather than being the name of a person, place, thing, action, or trait. We need not think of MPMs as smokers, actually, but I think it's safe to say they drink wine. They make the difference between the receptionist and the friend, between Siri and you. They bring language alive. Nor are MPMs usually as tough to specify as little *well*. They simply require us to expand our conception of what it is to "mean" something, especially since the fact that no one tells us about this side of language so often leads to misunderstandings about how people talk.

In putting a face on language, MPMs even lend themselves to a handy acronym, FACE, that allows us to explore how deeply this "secret" realm of language permeates our very beings. More specifically, the FACE schema gives us a sense of the perfectly ordinary place words have gone when, superficially, they seem to have gone off the rails because it's hard to nail down what they "mean." In English, MPMs can be classified according to four principal functions that they cluster around:

F: Factuality
A: Acknowledgment of others' state of mind
C: Counterexpectation
E: Easing

This likely seems a random set of distinctions. In fact, it constitutes quite a bit of what it is to actually talk—not speak or recite, but talk.

Factuality: For Real

The weather headline VERY COLD WEATHER NEXT WEEK is quite plausible, but REALLY COLD WEATHER NEXT WEEK sounds like *The Onion*, despite the fact that the two sentences have the same literal meaning. Yet we can't say that *really* is too slangy. Buttoned-up sorts say *really* all day long every day. *There isn't really a lake there; I'd really like to meet an ombudsman*—these sentences are hardly candidates for the Urban Dictionary.

What makes *really* seem out of place in a headline is that it is fundamentally emotional: it's too *personal*. We can sprinkle *really* all over a sentence to lend notes of personally backed insistence with an in-the-moment feel: *Really, I didn't even see the point of going outside when it was that hot; He wants to pay it in installments, but really, what's point of dragging it out?; I'm just tired of the whole mess, really.* Note that in all these cases, *in reality* would not convey the particular meaning that *really* does. The reason *I'm just tired of the whole mess, in reality* seems off is that *really* and *in reality* do not mean the same thing.

Really conveys a hand-on-the-heart testament, something individual in a way that *in reality* is not. In terms of the grand old Parts of Speech from our school days, *really* is often a kind of interjection. Formal language, as opposed to casual speech, is cooler, more objective, and thus *really* feels out of place in a news headline. "Really cold" would mean not only "very cold," but, in addition, that the degree of cold moves you, to the extent that you feel driven to point it out. *Really* is about your gut feelings in a way that *very* is much less so. *Really* comes coated in modal sauce.

But where does that coating come from? Why doesn't *really* simply mean "very" or "in reality"? Because some words get personal. *Really* is now so far from its origins in the word *real* that it doesn't even sound like its parent anymore. It's been uttered so often that it has melted into "rilly"—most of us realize the connection with *real* only as we learn to spell. *Really* is a tool: it less means something than *does* something. In peppering our casual speech with *really*, we give an ongoing kind of testament.

It's part of the fact that actual speech happens between live persons with needs and expectations. Part of an unspoken social contract with other persons is basic sincerity; language, naturally, reflects that. With *really* we ritually highlight the factuality of what we are saying, rather than simply making it and leaving it there, a practice that the impersonality of print allows more easily. *Really* flags our sincerity. The analogy is with how we perform a basic courtesy toward those we see regularly via asking, "How are you?" The reason we would often be almost offended to receive an actual answer is that, like *really*, "How are you?" *does*, rather than *means*, something.

Really, then, is a paradigm example of the *F* in FACE, the Factuality flavor of modal marker. The story of *really* has two parts, like a movie and its sequel. In the first installment, *really* was one of many English words meaning "truth" that came to mean *very*—such as *very* itself, which came from the French word for *true*, *vrai* (*verrai* in the late thirteenth century). *Very* is the well-worn version of *verily* just as "rilly" is what happens to *really* with heavy use. *Truly* was another example, of course, with *true* having undergone the same transformation as *verrai* a couple of centuries earlier. Even farther back there had been others. In the poem "The Owl and the Nightingale" of around 1200, the Middle English trips you up just as you think you're in good hands: *Ich was in one sumere dale . . ."* ("I was in a summer dale") *in one suthe digele hale*. What? *Digel* was an original English word for "secret"; *hale* is "hall," or, in a poetic sense, "space," "place." But *suthe*: the key to that one is perhaps clearer in the way it would later be spelled, *sooth*: it meant "truth," captured today only in *soothsayer*.* But *sooth* had an extended meaning as—you guessed it—"truly," or "very." *In one suthe digele hale* meant "in a very secluded place."

Very, true, and *sooth* show that when a word means "true" and it's used a lot, you can almost predict that, over time, it will glide from meaning "truth" into meaning "very." But the process can also go further than that, and that's where *really* comes in. *Very* settled into serving as an objective word, of the kind learners get in textbooks early on. But the personal pull got a hold of *really*, such that it morphed

---

* Unless you're given to saying *forsooth* beyond performing Shakespeare or occasionally being called upon to sing the old standard "Yesterdays." (My hat is off to singers who manage to sing "Joyous, free, and flaming life forsooth was mine," an almost willfully clammy lyric even for 1933.)

beyond the *very* stage into a more personal (i.e., modal) place. When someone says it's *really cold*, we think of them shivering under their coat, not a weather report. To say, *Okay, really, what are we going to do?* is to indicate one's emotional commitment to getting down to cases. You show your FACE.

A language needs factual modal markers of this kind; in English, the roll of the dice chose *really* for the job. Elsewhere, other stuff fills in. On the island of Sulawesi in Indonesia, best known elsewhere for its coffee, in one language called Seko Padang to say you're full you say *Kuboromo*. But to say what you mean in English by "I'm really full!" you say *Kuboromo-ko*. That little *ko*—wouldn't you know it's called a *veri*dical marker—does the job of *really* in English. The question is *how* a language will convey that nuance, not whether it will.

What happened to words like *very, true, sooth,* and *real* reveals that when a word means *truth*, we should expect that its meaning will eventually shift: what would be strange is if it didn't. A word is something that goes, not sits, and the very meaning of truth is ripe for transformation into related concepts such as intensification and extremity, including the fate of *really*, which we might call an example of factuality maintenance.

Literally, then, is easy. It was originally one more variation on indicating truth—specifically exactness, as in "by the letter": *He took the advice literally; He meant it literally.* But that can have been only a snapshot along a time line; there was never any question that *literally* was going to morph into other meanings. The only question was what kind. For one, *literally* quite predictably went beyond its original meaning into one where "by the letter" no longer makes sense except as a metaphor: *We were literally the only ones there; We were literally on the brink of a depression.* There are no letters involved in these statements, but *literally* means that the statement is true in a specific way—as in what we sometimes even refer to as "by the letter."

A next step was for *literally* to go personal, on a mission less to specify than to vent. This is when we use *literally* to attest to the vividness of our personal sentiments amid plainly exaggerated, fantastical metaphors during animated storytelling, justifications, and the like. *I was literally dying of thirst and she wouldn't give me any water* is not intended to mean that someone really was perishing, but that they truly were experiencing what that expression does connote, extreme thirst. *I literally coined money*—that is, I indeed was making *quite* a bit of money. Here is factuality again, flagging sincerity. The personal pull, ever present, had its eternal effect: like *really*, like *literally*.

Or not. Online comments sections overflow with declamations about the "misuse" of *literally*. The idea would seem to be that, for one, *literally* must not be extended into metaphorical usage beyond a certain minimal point. *He took the advice literally* is okay, because though oral advice does not properly have letters, we might take "letters" to refer to language in general. But at a sentence like Vice President Joseph Biden's *The country was literally on the brink of a depression,* toleration stops, out of an objection that one cannot be on the brink of something "by the letter." And then all hell breaks loose over the use of *literally* in sentences such as *I was so sick, I was literally dying and she still expected me to come to work.* The educator and lexicographer H. W. Fowler, in his grand guide to usage, groaned in 1926, "We have come to such a pass with this emphasizer that where the truth would require us to insert with a strong expression 'not literally, of course, but in a manner of speaking,' we do not hesitate to insert the very word that we ought to be at pains to repudiate." The acidic satirist and journalist Ambrose Bierce in 1909 had declared similarly that "to affirm the truth of the exaggeration is intolerable." As I write, one can actually purchase a T-shirt emblazoned, MISUSE OF LITERALLY MAKES ME FIGURATIVELY INSANE.

But ultimately, in view of the fact that language inherently goes rather than sits, *literally* is that kid in sixth grade who became the one to make fun of for some random reason when, with another roll of the dice, many of his tormentors would have been equally ripe for torment and what everybody really deserved was to be left alone. More to the point, *literally* is that kid subjected to a bizarre accusation that he is remiss in refusing to talk and dress like his grandfather.

A first clue that we need a more realistic take on *literally* is that neither Bierce nor Fowler has been with us for quite some time. The person calling in to a radio show will complain about how people are using *literally* "lately" when, after all, Bierce and Fowler were writing when movies were silent. The nonliteral uses of *literally* are quite traditional, of all things. *Literally* had gone past meaning "by the letter" in any sense as early as the eighteenth century, when, for example, Francis Brooke wrote *The History of Emily Montague* (1769), which contains this sentence: "He is a fortunate man to be introduced to such a party of fine women at his arrival; it is literally to feed among the lilies." One cannot feed among anything "by the letter." Or, in 1806, when the philosopher David Hume wrote, "He had the singular fate of dying literally of hunger," in his signature history of England, despite the fact that there are no letters via which to starve. Yet this was an authoritative and highly popular volume, more widely read at the time than Hume's philosophical treatises, equivalent to modern histories by Simon Schama and Peter Ackroyd. The purely figurative usage is hardly novel, either: the sentence *I literally coined money* was written by Fanny Kemble in 1863. Kemble, a British stage actress, hardly considered herself a slangy sort of person.

Of course, some could object that just because people were doing it a long time ago doesn't mean they were any more correct than we are. But a second clue about *literally* is a certain inconsistency in objections to its figurative usage. Fowler suggested *practically* as a substitute, but in its usage as "approximately," *practically* has drifted into a near opposite to *practical*'s original meanings of "actual," "realistic," and "suitable," has it not? Also, it's easy to forget how far even the meanings of *very* and *truly* are from where they began. *It all made my daughter very happy*—try paraphrasing that with "in actuality," the original meaning of *verrai* and *truly*. "It all made my daughter happy in actuality"? What—in comparison to her alternate happinesses in the fifth dimension? Or, where are the pedants opining that *very*'s original, and therefore "real," meaning is *verily*, and that

therefore to call something very small implies that something else could be *unverily* small?

Thus in some cases we have no problem with words'
meanings drifting quite a bit. Yet, finally, some might still
object that the figurative is the *direct opposite* of "by the letter." Surely there's something particularly irregular about
that? But in fact there isn't, which is our third clue that hat-
ing on the new *literally* is like daring a lava lamp not to let
its clump drift into "improper" configurations on the pain
of being disconnected. If *fast* means "speedy," then why can
you hold fast and be fast asleep? And did it ever bother
you? *Dusting* can be removing something (like dust) or laying it down (like fertilizer or paprika). No T-shirts about that.
You *seed* a watermelon to get the seeds out, but when you
seed the soil you're putting the seeds in. You can *bolt* from a
room (running fast) in which the chairs are bolted to the
floor (stuck fast).

Examples go on and on—and notice they matter not a
jot. They're called contronyms, and the only reason nobody
goes around with a shirt reading, AGAINST THE MISUSE OF
FAST TO MEAN "RAPID" I SIT STEADFAST, is that the bifurca-
tion happened before there were people thinking of English
words as held *fast* in dictionaries. The question is: do contronyms actually create ambiguity, or are they construed as
possibly creating ambiguity via willful overanalysis? Asked
to seed a watermelon, no one carefully removes the seeds
from one watermelon and then inserts them into another
one. Genuine ambiguity disturbs like a stray eyelash. I once
had occasion to spend hours in a hospital where the nurses
often referred to *discharge*. They usually meant the process

of someone being given leave to depart the premises, but sometimes they meant the less savory orifice-related meaning of the word. In that context, the difference mattered, and I was repeatedly confused for a flicker as to which meaning they intended, including an odd ten seconds in which I sincerely thought one nurse was talking about something I'd best not dwell upon when she was actually talking about insurance papers to sign before leaving.

Who among us can say that the figurative use of *literally* occasions confusion of this kind? It never does—perfect, idiomatic comprehension thrives because context always makes clear which meaning is intended. Language is not self-standing orations howled into the ether; it is a vehicle for talking about life and emotions directly experienced, recalled, or predicted from moment to moment. Too often we are taught to think about language as if it were written sentences out of a Language Arts workbook. Walter Ong, in his magnificent book on the difference between oral and written uses of language, magnificently got across why this is a mistake:

> Written words are isolated from the fuller context in which spoken words come into being. The word in its natural, oral habitat is a part of a real, existential present. Spoken utterance is addressed by a real, living person to another real, living person or real, living persons, at a specific time in a real setting which includes always much more than mere words. Spoken words are always modifications of a total situation which is more than verbal. They never occur alone, in a context simply of words.

Few would have any argument with Ong here, and most might even see him as belaboring the obvious. However, if so, then equally obvious is that even contronyms create no cognitive dissonance. The richness of context keeps miscomprehension from even having a chance to begin.

In that light, the fact that *literally* can mean both itself and its opposite is—admit it—cool! The way *literally* now works is a quirky, chance development of the kind that makes one quietly proud to speak a language. It's neat that *fast* can mean both fleet and sitting tight. I for one *like* that something can both weather away and also weather a storm, in one instance destroyed and in the other, holding *fast*. Or at least, I'd be hard-pressed to say it hurts anything. A perfectly reasonable (and in Hume's charming spelling, "chearful") perspective on *literally* is that we were watching to see where this word was going and—get this—it ended up meaning its own opposite!

Literally, then, is just one more factuality marker amid the FACEs of English. Words move; there are new factual markers a-borning as I write. One of them is almost perfect: *straight up*, as in I *straight up told her she had to move out*. It has the personal, "I'm telling you" function of *really* and of the figurative *literally*, and given that factuality markers come from words referring to truth, it's no surprise that this is exactly what *straight up*'s original meaning is: one can also mean it to say, essentially, *I agree*. Wouldn't you know, *true* and *tree* developed from the same ancient word: Millennia ago, English speakers saw trustworthiness in the straight-up quality of trees. The rest was history, which has that famous way of repeating itself: today people are feeling the same trustworthiness in the expression *straight up* itself.

Acknowledgment: I Hear You

Thus speaking is about more than making tidy little observations about things and concepts, what they do, and what they're like. Notice that the only humans who talk this way are toddlers, from whom it sounds cute—as in, less than mature. Running alongside the "blackboard" realm of language is another one, through which we communicate our feelings about what we're saying not just with facial expressions and gestures, but with speech. With the factuality wing of the FACE apparatus, we prophylactically attest to sincerity. Something else we do as humans, rather than robots, is routinely acknowledge others' state of mind. It is, fundamentally, a kind of politeness, although less overt than deliberately taught formulas such as saying "Please" and "Thank you." And just as with factual markers like *really* and *literally*, a "parts of speech" view of language misses the true function of our Acknowledgment tools. These tools lurk in places you'd never suspect, of a kind that many consider suspicious indeed. Yet English wouldn't be a human language without them.

An example is, of all things, the word *totally*, as used by young (and, increasingly, "younger") people. *He's totally going to call you* means neither "He is going to call you in a total fashion" nor even "He is actually going to call you."

Anyone who uses *totally* in this way or hears it often will intuit that it has a more specific meaning than *actually*. *He is actually going to call you* would mean simply "It turns out that he will call, despite what you thought." *He's totally going to call you* is much more specific: it refers to feelings between you and the person you are talking to. *He's totally going to call you*: you and I both know that someone has said otherwise, or that the chances of it may seem slim at first glance, but in fact, the naysayers are wrong, and whoo-hoo, he is going to call!

Totally tracks and nods to the opinions of others with an air of warm fellow feeling. It's no surprise that it has become entrenched enough to be clipped to the cheery *Totes!* (which surely does not mean "Completely!"). *It's totally gonna snow* implies that someone said it wouldn't, or that there would be only flurries, and also that you and the person you say this to are in some way in the same boat as to how that heavy snow is going to affect you. If someone in Chicago turned on the TV and caught the tail end of a newscast in which someone said, "It's totally going to snow," you know they would have tuned in to a local station, not a national show covering weather conditions across the nation. The *totally* wouldn't "read" coherently from someone likely too far away to experience the snowstorm themselves, because *totally* is about shared sentiment: once again, what looks like slack-jawed devolution actually contains a degree of sophistication.

Here is where little *well* fits in, acknowledging what someone has said (i.e., what they think) while nicely venturing an additive or correction. Someone says, *That Thomas the Train is cool, isn't he?* The proper response is *Well, frankly, no—I find him rather strangely dull; I prefer the Powerpuff Girls.* Note: one would not respond *Frankly, no—I find him rather strangely dull; I prefer the Powerpuff Girls.* The absence of *well* may seem a small distinction but isn't; the *well* makes the difference between a normal exchange and a zinger, likely delivered in an old play or to be deliberately arch.

Acknowledgment also takes forms beyond what we typically think of as words. In language, it helps to think of *word* as an approximate notion. Quite often, a phrase of two or more words does what one word could easily do. *Never mind!*, for example, is two words technically, but the *never* is not meant literally. You aren't warning someone to "never" think about something over time, but to not think about it right now, and *mind*, in the meaning of "attend to," is actually close to archaic beyond a few expressions. We barely stop to think what the words in *Never mind!* actually mean— rather, *Never mind!* is in essence a single "word" in itself, such that we are not surprised to know that for the same concept, Russians use the one word *nothing*. Other examples include *Forget about it* (not accidentally spelled as the single word *Fuhgeddaboudit* in New Yorkese) and *Long story short* for "To make a long story short."

Or, *and stuff.* Here is a shaggy bit of speech we associate with imprecision, but it can be seen another way. Again, it's no novelty—English speakers turn up using it even in formal documents as far back as the 1620s, as in someone investigating a rather grisly prison and finding "six several Priests prisoners in several Chambers, and Altar, with all Furniture thereto belonging, with Church-Books and Stuff."

Part of the joy of the novel *Middlemarch* is how you can almost smell the characters from nearly two centuries' remove, and one of my favorite facets of that is that George Eliot has Dorothea Brooke's dilettante uncle speak with an *and that kind of thing* tic: "Life isn't cast in a mould—not cut out by rule and line and that sort of thing," "You are not fond of show, a great establishment, balls, dinners, that kind of thing," "I lunched there and saw Casaubon's library, and that kind of thing." This shows that there were people who used that expression in that way, so familiar to us now, even in the mid-nineteenth century, when Eliot wrote.

For Mr. Brooke, to be sure, that little expression ends up helping kill his political chances, as he retains it even when giving a public address and a heckler parrots it back at him. Few would classify *and stuff* or *and that kind of thing* as appropriate to formal speech, but the informal is not always incoherent. *And stuff* and its equivalents reflect a visit into other people's heads, the assumption being that the things not being specified are known already, such that one need not take the time to elaborate. "You are not fond of show, a great establishment, balls, dinners, that kind of thing"—Brooke is envisioning a scene and assumes we, prompted by the basics, have approximately the same picture in our heads, with not only balls and dinners but certain kinds of dancing, clothing, manners, pit odor, faintings, and delusions. With *and that kind of thing*, Brooke is drawing upon an assumed common body of knowledge among the kinds of people he talks to most—the matter is intimate, personal.

Warm, even. *Stuff like that there* is another variant, and an old song of that title has the lyric "I want some huggin' and some squeezin' and some muggin' and some teasin' and some stuff like that there"—we all know what "stuff" the singer is referring to, especially in 1945, when a popular song could go only so far in specifying such things. There can be a cozy wink in it, vividly apparent in today's robust vernacular variant *'n' shit*. Because it involves the word *shit* one might dismiss this simply as "profanity," but that's like calling a fire blazing in a living room hearth a high-temperature oxidation. Profane *'n' shit* may be, but it also summons shared knowledge. After all, a home fire isn't just a chemical process; it's cozy *'n' shit*. By that, do I mean that it is both comfortable and a kind of feces? No: I mean that it is cozy, with all the associations we have with coziness, many of which may challenge expression—it's probably nighttime, you're probably with someone you like, it's a nice way to end a day, it has a gamy smell modern life usually doesn't expose us much to, it might get one in mind for, say, stuff like that there. You don't have to say all that; it's all implied by *'n' shit*.

It is here, then, that *you know* fits in. It is one more acknowledgment marker, typical of what any living language needs, and predictable as the fate of a word *know* when acknowledgment markers are all about what the other person . . . knows. *You know* can sound like verbal litter, and indeed one can lean on it excessively to compensate for being unsure of what to say. However, to never use it would suggest an oddly self-directed communicator. To say *you know* is to take a quick trip into your interlocutor's mind, this time in order to facilitate your presentation of a point by suggesting that the other person knew what you know all the time. One can even use it when that shared perspective seems unlikely: *That bus is, you know, the last one for the night*—in that even implying that the person knew what you know seems less pedantic than just laying the point out straight. As one linguist perfectly nailed *you know*, it lends a "pretense of shared knowledge that achieves intimacy"— i.e., we're again in the FACE world. Note that he said "pretense," just as another linguist who is great on *you know* put it that it is "presenting new information as if it were old information in order to improve its reception."

You know is handy in showing that classifying all these words and expressions as acknowledgment markers is not some kind of special pleading for linguistic sloth. *You know* goes way back—if it's lazy to say *you know*, then English speakers have been lazy since, say, Chaucer's time, when he has his *Canterbury Tales* characters popping off with *you knows* and similar things, like *thow woost*, where *woost* is the old *know* verb, which otherwise spawned the *wit* in *mother wit* and *use your wits*. Emily in "The Knight's Tale" says, *I am, thow woost, yet of thy compaignye a mayde, and love huntynge and venerye*, with *thow woost* as *you know* for the fourteenth century.

And it had been ever thus: *Beowulf*, that masterpiece in Old English, is a little weird in its very first word—since when does an epic poem begin with "What!"? Yet generations of scholars have internalized that first line *Hwæt! We gardena in geardagum þeodcyninga þrym gefrunon*... "What! We have heard of the fame of the spear-Danes' people-kings..." Really, though? Did Old English speakers kick off a good tale by bleating "Whaat!" to quiet everybody down? Actually, no. Many translators have gotten by the awkwardness by using *Lo!* but even that doesn't get across what that *What* actually meant. The original manuscripts have no punctuation; that was added later, by editors. In manuscript, the passage is simply HWÆT WE GARDENA IN GEARDAGUM. There is no indication that *hwæt* was an interjection kicking off the show, and from how *hwæt* is used throughout Old English documents in general, we can see that it actually translates best as roughly "So . . ." In the *Beowulf* opening, for example, it brought the listener or reader in, with an implication that the fame of the spear-Danes' kings was familiar, reinforcing that it was something of which "we have heard." Imagine: "So we've heard of the spear-Danes' people-kings' fame." *Hwæt*, then, went into the audience's mind: in Old English, *what* could be used as an acknowledgment marker.

A language has so many ways of doing things: conveying not just meaning but attitude, packing a concept into not just one word but two or three—or, even, expressing a concept in ways beyond words. Intonation, for instance, communicates so very much beyond broad emotions. Just as there is many a slip between a word's original meaning and what it can come to mean—*literally* 1.0 and *literally* 2.0, or *what* meaning "so"—intonation can come to mean something other than what we're trained to suppose.

Why, for example, do younger people seem to be asking questions when they're making statements? *So it was Daylight Savings Time? And I forgot to set my clocks back? And so I got to school late and Anderson gave me extra homework?* Those observations could seem more gracefully couched as declarations. Why are these people so unsure? To the extent that women have been documented to be more likely to use what has been called uptalk, we might read this as evidence that they lack conviction, and perhaps that uptalk is a linguistic response to sexist dismissal.

Tempting ideas, but actually what we're seeing is that the meaning of an intonation can drift, via implication, just as the meaning of a word can. This includes questions. It's interesting how often what we couch formally as questions are actually meant as statements. If we ask someone who is piling their omelette with pepper "How much pepper do you *need*?" we are not waiting for them to specify how much. We are stating something, and something quite specific: that the person is overdoing it—here, using too much pepper. Languages are full of wrinkles, and here is one, where the meaning clashes with the form. One way of calling someone out on some kind of excess is to phrase it in the form of that particular *how* question: *How cold do you need it to be?* (It's now too cold), *How many times do I have to tell you?* (I've told you too many times as of now). Convention and context ensure that this confuses no one, which is why a language allows such things to creep in and settle.

Uptalk is another example of the question form used to convey declaration. If the uptalker is actually questioning anything, it is not the validity of her statement but whether the person listening understands or shares the same basis of knowledge and evaluations. However, in performing that question so often, she is not spastically seeking endless answers and validation despite already holding the privilege of being the one holding the conversational floor. In its use in uptalk, the questioning intonation has morphed into a passing gesture: it doesn't *mean*; it *does*—namely, it ongoingly establishes that you and the other person are on the same page.

That's a natural evolution from questioning, just as *y'know* is a natural evolution from the verb "to know." In uptalk, questioning has become even more personal than it already is. In uptalking, you are acknowledging (Acknowledging) the interlocutor's state of mind. In that, to uptalk is actually quite nice, in the grand scheme of things. Or, as certain people would put it, "Uptalk is nice?" Those comfortably dismissive of potshots against youthspeak might even put it as "Uptalk is totally nice."

Counterexpectation: Much to My Surprise

To glean articulateness in sentences like those may feel a tad queer, but the sense of dislocation is worth it. To understand FACE is to see a great deal of language in a different, and less depressing, way. Just as geneticists are learning that ever more of what has been dismissed as "junk" DNA has purpose, a great deal of what feels like the trash in English is part of how the language gets basic work done.

When we use little *even* to indicate disapproval or surprise, for example, it becomes part of the Counterexpectational component of FACE. *He didn't even bring a present*—i.e., despite that one expected he would. Counterexpectation isn't something we learn in school as central to grammar: we learn about the future tense and predicates and objects. But languages quite eagerly corral words (and more) into conveying counterexpectation as well. It's part of being human to sort out what's everyday and what's new, and a big part of communication is, after all, to remark upon what's new.

Take *actually*, which became a counterexpectation marker instead of taking the factuality route that *really* took. *Actually* started, as we would expect, with its "dictionary" meaning "in reality." But by the eighteenth century, speakers were also using it for a judgmental (i.e., personal) function. *He actually killed the cat*: note you can barely say that without making some kind of FACE.

But you never know how a language is going to convey the counterexpectation part of the FACE apparatus. There are any number of ways a language gets across the "Hey!" sentiment beyond its mere word for *Hey*. In English, profanity plays its role here, too, this time with the word *ass*. There is a *big pot* and there is a *big-ass pot*, there is a *lame excuse* and a *lame-ass excuse*. An initial temptation is to think this is simply a matter of profanity. However, that implies that leaving aside the fact that one of them is rude, *big pot* and *big-ass pot* have the same meaning. They don't.

You can tell from really trying to imagine just any old adjective, any old time, quietly appended with *-ass*. Even in the most foulmouthed person you can imagine, notice how hard it is to imagine him saying, *I saw a gray-ass squirrel*. If you think about it, he'd say that only if he thought of squirrels of some other color as normal, such that the gray squirrel is a surprise. *Gray-ass squirrel* comes with a backstory:

"Where I come from, squirrels are black, but when I got here, I looked out the window and saw a gray-ass squirrel!"

Gray-ass doesn't mean simply "gray as uttered by a potty-mouth," but "counterexpectationally gray." This is why another possible intuition actually doesn't go through, that *big-ass* means "really big" compared to just big, such that there might be a profane parallel grammar:

POLITE	NAUGHTY
big	big
bigger	big-ass
biggest	biggest

But to remark on the pot being "really big" implies, in itself, that there was an expectation that it would not be. Otherwise, the overlap between *big-ass* and just neutral *bigger* alone is actually quite partial. *Willa is big, Wesley is bigger, and Brian is the biggest*—in no parallel grammar could you recast this as "Willa is big, Wesley is big-ass, and Brian is the biggest." And forget "You can yell, but I'll yell loud-ass-(ly?)" (or "Air is light-ass than water"!).

Words change, and *ass* was assigned a mission. A good guess is that it started with *big-ass*, because in language as in so much else, things tend to start with the literal and drift into the abstract, and human beings can literally have large behinds: *Then a big-ass fellow jumped in and settled it once and for all*. However, yes, it would have been *fellow* rather than *guy, dude,* or *bro,* because the counterexpectational *ass* floated beyond anatomical plausibility as far back as 1919, when someone was documented as getting angry when a "silly ass barber shaved my neck." All manner of -*ass* usages pop up well before 1950: an accent criticized as having "lousy broad-ass As," and familiar-sounding locutions such as *green-ass* (corporals), *poor-ass* (southerners), and *broke-ass* (a waiter). In all these cases, the point is that the quality in question draws attention.*

In narrating, we are creating a little movie. We need to focus the camera or the lights on what we deem worthy of note. We don't want to only show a waiter, but to remark that he was broke, since it isn't considered the norm for someone who works to be broke. A real camera could zero in on his frayed cuffs or show him hitching a ride home: in a grand old film noir, the character would not be written as actually stating, "I lack funds." Talking, we might designate the waiter as *broke-ass*: "He was working and all, but actually he didn't have any money."

---

* Of course, in some cases, the meaning of -*ass* with particular adjectives has gone on to freeze into something more neutral. *Smart-ass* presumably began as meaning "unexpectedly smart-mouthed" but now means simply "sassy"—although *sassy* itself contains an element of the counter-expectational: it's a personality that confronts one and goes against the preferred norm. Similarly, *wise-ass* would have begun as meaning unexpectedly, and probably unpleasantly, smart, and froze into its current meaning of, again, "sassy, derisive." This kind of thing happens when grammar gets old: meanings get more idiosyncratic and specific. *Sloth* started as "slow-th" meaning slowness. The sound change from "oh" to "aw" is a sign that the word has been around a good long time, and during that much time, it is natural that *sloth* drifted into meaning something much more specific than just "slowness." We'll learn more about this kind of change in chapter 2.

The reconception of the *derrière* is but one of the odd ways you can see languages conveying life's counterintuitive aspects. In Saramaccan, spoken in the rain forest of Surinam, there is a difference between "dried fish" and "dried-dried fish," but it isn't that the latter refers to hideously dessicated fish; nor is it some kind of baby talk. "Dried fish" is fish that is traditionally eaten dried, along the lines of what Westerners are usually most familiar with from northern European smoked fish or assorted Japanese snacks. "Dried-dried fish" would be fish of any kind accidentally left out in the sun, or deliberately dried out despite usually being served fresh: dry *against expectation*. Or, in a language of Nepal called Kham, to say, *Hey, look, he took them!*, you put it as "His taking of them, its existence!" I suspect if America spent a summer expressing surprise that way it would feel natural by around October, but I'm not holding my breath. Meanwhile, we'll always have *ass*.

Easing: No Worries

The final component of FACE is Easing. Much of what we do when speaking is devoted to ensuring a basic comfort level, which is unsurprising given that many scholars have seen exactly this as a primary component of what it is to be polite.

The sheer amount of laughter in typical conversation, including not just guffaws but chuckles and little passing jokes, is counterintuitive under a view of speech as just "communication." Human speech is a laughy-ass business:

we prefer communication within an ongoing reassurance that there is no impending social threat, that everyone is on the same page. A person who never laughs or chuckles lacks charm; you're never quite comfortable with such a person, and you suspect they don't like you. Anthropologists even have a name for this decorative kind of laughter that you miss only when it isn't there: Duchenne laughter. It follows that shared sense of humor is so often the spark and sustenance for a romantic relationship, the most intimate and therefore most potentially dangerous kind. "Why Paul and not Andrew? I don't know . . . he made me laugh." The core essence of laughter is as a jolly manifestation of amusement, but because the state of mutual laughter is inherently relaxing and bonding, in conversation laughter is less *at* something than *for* something. It has become a quiet but potent tool.

This easing function percolates into language itself, upon which the nature of texting's abbreviation LOL ends up making perfect sense. Originally it meant "laughing out loud," and was used to indicate that one was genuinely and directly amused by a comment. However, quickly LOL came to be sprinkled throughout text exchanges with a frequency far beyond anything that would make sense as amusement. A popular article floats the idea that LOL has no real meaning at all by exemplifying its usage in a wide range of sentences.

However, when people have a hard time assigning a "meaning" to something they nevertheless produce day in and day out, it's a clue that we're on to something in the *pragmatic* wing of language, where we have to get used to a different sense of what something means—namely, it's where words *do* rather than "mean." A goodly sampling of the sentences from the LOL article:

I like you. Im pretty sure everyone else figured that out before you lol

I dunno, just assuming? I wasn't sure if you did lol but I guess I shouldn't assume

They charged me again so it wont cancel for a while lol

Oh lol yea they charged me again but only for a month

No way lol it was just a question

That is different and now you know I actually like you and not just sex like lol

I feel like you think that's a bad thing lol

Ahh ok—lol. I wanted to ask you if you would drive me to the airport :)

Nope, not for the next couple of weeks. Why, ya miss me??? lol

lol rude.

Lol . . . not even . . . you miss me?

(Sleepy?) Lol a lil bit

Do u think its possible To fall in love at first Skype?! Lol

Maybe lol

The LOLs in those passages are certainly prolific, but not devoid of function. All LOLs take the edge off. They buffer the uncertainties and vulnerabilities of, for example, burgeoning romance, as we sense from the content. The *lol*s are typeset chuckles, of exactly the kind you can hear in vocal conversation.

LOL has morphed from something direct and broad into something more abstractly subjective than guffawing at a joke. "Laughing out loud" now applies to LOL only as an origin story; anyone who used LOL to signal actual laughter would now be misunderstood: it would be, quite simply, a mistake. Texting, as speech of a sort, needs modal particles, and develops them from promising materials. Just as *genuinely* now does the job that *very* once did in its *verily* period, today one uses other acronyms such as LMAO ("laughing my ass off") to indicate actual laughter, because LOL has moved on.

More obviously, expressions such as *I know, right?*, which can sound like tics, are serving the same easing function, this time in terms of indicating agreement. To simply state that you agree over and over again would ease no one, suggesting perhaps an impending and unwelcome embrace. "I agree. I agree. I agree." There needs to be a more easing way to communicate such a thing, and recurrent *I know, right?* serves the function, in that those words indicate agreement readably, but more obliquely.

As always, English is just being a language: easing markers are not traceable to something about being a modern American. When I was learning German, I recall a friend offering me a bite of an apple with *Magst mal abbissen?* Now, just *Magst abbissen?*—literally "Want to bite?"—would have been the textbook sentence, but there was that little word *mal.* I had learned it as meaning basically "time" or "one time," but had never heard it used the way my friend did; it sounded like she was specifying that I was restricted to biting it only once, which seemed incommensurate with the gleam in her eye. But walking away, from the context I sensed that the *mal* was a way of minimizing, creating a comfort zone: *Magst mal abbissen?* means "Want to bite a little?" or, more idiomatically, "Wanna little bite?" It isn't hard to imagine how "one time" came to mean "a little" or "just," as in *Just try it on.* One learns *mal* in learning to speak the language as opposed to reading it. It's a classic modal marker, in this case a softener; it eases. A word that means something as neutral as "time" ends up being a little *personal* tool to create an aura of coziness. Germans often use it where in English we might talk in a higher voice: you offer someone an apple without meaning to seem too pushy—quite possibly you will say Wanna *bite*? And if you are a person of a particular sort of sonic expressiveness, even just kind of squeak the melody of that sentence on a little grunty buzz: nn^{nhh}? And when people say such things, note also the raised eyebrows.

Then we perform the easing function in ways beyond mere words, which predictably occasions considerable confusion. For example, for those whose speech repertoire includes an informal variety considerably different from the formal one, the very act of switching into that informal variety with a fellow speaker of it is a gesture of easing. To speak the vernacular, the "dialect," the "just talking" kind of language, brings forward a shared identity as people who have the ability to speak in that way, and therefore creates a feeling of intimacy. The conversation becomes more comfortable just as it does with punctuations of laughter; it puts people at their ease.

In America, this is how Black English fits in, especially for more educated speakers. Black English began as a transformation of English by African slaves. They transformed English for two reasons. One: they learned the language working alongside indentured Irish, Scots-Irish, and lower-class British servants who spoke regional dialects of English rather than the standard. Two: adults don't learn languages as completely as children, and so naturally these slaves shaved off some of the quirks of English here and there. Today, a great many black Americans have full access to Standard English, and speak it with ease. However, Black English survives for them nevertheless. What was the only reality for their distant ancestors has now become a way to express facets of their personhood: Black English is a way of getting personal.

Thus often today Black English is a vehicle of *modal* expression. More specifically, it is an easing—the way that one signals warm connection, group membership. Black English for such speakers is not something they would ever speak continuously the way a less-educated Bavarian might spend most of his life speaking Bavarian rather than High German. Scholars of Black English seek and prize recordings of anyone speaking full-blown Black English for minutes on end the way some cherish bootleg tapes of Springsteen or Dylan.

For most black Americans when talking to one another, in addition to the battery of pragmatic strategies all English speakers have at their disposal, switching into Black English is ever available as a supplement. The very act of the switch is, in itself, an expression of empathy analogous to LOL. Hence the common sentiment that in many of its renditions, Black English is more honest, warmer, realer—there is feeling in it. "There Isn't Any Mountain High Enough" would never have made the charts; "Ain't No Mountain High Enough" is the necessary title for a song intended to convey heartfelt affection. Feeling could be considered the very essence of what Black English is for, to most modern black Americans who use it. It is part of the FACE component of speech.

Yet it is because Black English is often today a matter of the *pragmatic* realm of speaking that the black American fluent in Black English, apprised that she "speaks a dialect," is typically somewhat perplexed or even, due to the stigma attached to the dialect in some quarters, offended. Scholars see that stigma itself as responsible for the perplexity and ignorance. There is truth there, but the person who feels something off in the idea that they speak a "thing" called Black English is nevertheless onto something. The idea of a Rosetta Stone set for Ebonics seems silly for a reason: Black English does not feel like a discrete dialect of English in the way that Sicilian is a dialect of Italian (or, as analyzed by many, not even properly "Italian" at all). To most speakers, Black English feels like a repertoire one takes advantage of, a tool kit—"something you can dip into," as it is often put. They're right, and although they have no reason to put it this way, it's because, for them, Black English is a *pragmatic* strategy.

For that reason, a great many of the grammatical traits

documented as part of Black English are more FACE components (pragmatic) than vanilla semantic items familiar to all English speakers such as using -er to mark the comparative and -s to make something plural. We have seen the *straight up* factuality marker. The *yo* used before or after a sentence, as in *Dat's my jam, yo!* (where *jam* refers to a popular song, not something to spread on bread), is an acknowledgment marker. Distinct from the *Yo!* used to call someone, this *yo* is uttered in a parenthetical way, and summons common feeling: *Dat's my jam, yo!* translates roughly as "That is my favorite song, comrades!" with an assumption that it's a lot of your friends' favorite song, too—you wouldn't say it if you happened to be into Scriabin, or some odd little song you knew was just a quirky personal favorite of yours. Or, when a black person says, *She done growed up*, he doesn't simply mean "She grew up." That *done* is used only when the observation is counterexpectational. *She done growed up!* conveys that you find it counterintuitive that the little girl you seem to have encountered just a couple of years ago is now driving a car.

And then, easing is the very use of the dialect at all. There are those who criticize Barack Obama for using elements of Black English when he addresses black audiences. They see the switch as fake, from someone they usually hear speaking Standard English. To understand Black English as a modal gesture clarifies the matter: Obama's Black English is the texter's LOL.

The FACE of Humanity

The FACE part of English, then, is what allows us to talk rather than speak. Its components are each expressions of a fundamental aspect of being human. The philosopher of language Paul Grice outlined a Cooperative Principle of conversation, long accepted as canonical, under which we subconsciously follow certain maxims in an exchange. One is a commitment to truth: "Do not say what you believe to be false." Hence the reflex of underlining that one is sincere with factuality markers, driven also by another maxim that encourages one to be maximally informative—we want our interlocutors to know we're giving them the real deal. Then, to be human is to have a theory of mind, understanding the states of mind of people other than ourselves. Hence the acknowledgment impulse, which in the larger sense grows out of the fact that conversation is fundamentally a cooperation, not two people taking turns expressing themselves individually. It is, as the language evolution theorist Michael Tomasello has noted, not a matter of me talking to you and you talking to me but us communicating with each other.

Counterexpectation attracts such attention when we talk because of the simple fact that language is all about subjects and predicates, where a sentence does not function just to identify something (*Houseplant!*) but to say something about it (*That plant seems to have died*). Whatever you say about something is presumably novel to some degree, justifying the effort required to talk about it and taking up someone's time in sharing the observation with them. Even beyond the modal marker realm, much of language hinges on the difference between what is already known and what is new. The very difference between saying *that guy over there* and referring to him as *he* is that if you say *he*, then the person that *he* refers to is something already known. Counter-expectation, as in surprise, is merely a heightened manifestation of that basic new-old axis, where you highlight what you *personally* find to especially stand out against the expected.

Finally, easing is central to classic descriptions of how politeness works. To a large extent, politeness is a matter of making people comfortable, and key to that is taking things down a notch. The psychologist Roger Brown and the English literature scholar Albert Gilman classically described the transformation in accepted manners in Europe, where politeness came to allow ever more use of informal pronouns like the French *tu* rather than referring to single persons in the plural with words like *vous*, as if they were kings calling themselves "we." The comfort of solidarity triumphed over the chilliness of hierarchy. Or despite a sense one might have that politeness is about formal practices such as standing up straight, saying "please," and wearing proper attire, the linguist Robin Lakoff nailed that seeking degrees of informality is also a basic element in what it is to be polite.

The lesson from the FACE paradigm, however, is not only a matter of plugging assorted locutions into slots representing the human essence. The issue is: how do words end up in those slots? Clearly no one makes them up on the fly. Instead, words start out in what we think of as normal meanings, and then morph into ones that fit into FACE slots. It's a regular process, one of the many normal fates of words.

It can seem that what happens to words is either their sounds wear off—"Did you eat?" Becomes "Jeet?"—or they veer off into a semantic gutter, stuttered vaguely by people unconcerned with precision, such as how *totally* can sound and how LOL looks. However, the real story is richer, and we have seen the first part of it with FACE: one thing that has happened to words in all languages since there ever was language is that they have moved from objective to subjective. *Rather* starts as "early" and becomes "preferably," or the process can go even further and yield a word that has no meaning other than conveying some facet of subjectivity we need to get across, often hard even to describe as a "meaning." That's *you know, big-ass, LOL,* and even the figurative *literally* that gets into so many people's trash. These words do not encounter a semantic gutter; *rather*, they pass into the elegant and indispensable softness of pragmatic butter.

Let's FACE It: Emoticons and the Fate of the Language

FACE makes sense of things, then. One last one: to understand that language has a modal component answers common questions as to whether emoticons are "taking over" written English, or whether it could be possible to write only in emoticons. Those questions are based on an assumption that emoticons are mere decorations upon a writing system that was complete without them. However, it wasn't. Emoticons are not taking over, but filling a hole. They provide something that was missing from texting language at first: the pragmatic part.

Texting, in that it is casual, rapid, and vernacular, is executed via the physical process of writing, but is actually better described as a written kind of speech. As we have seen, speech differs from formal language in its being couched in personal feelings, eternally demonstrated alongside the more concrete communication of content. It was inevitable, then, that once texting became the staff of life for a generation, its users would quickly start developing ways of injecting texts with the warmth of humanity in a way that, for example, the formality of telexing or faxing did not encourage.*

But of course, emoticons could no more constitute a language by themselves than we could speak exclusively modally with no actual content. Writing all in emoticons would largely be the equivalent of saying, *Well, anyway I mean, totally, you know.* To the extent that this sentence is at all plausible, it could be so only after previous sentences that had established actual content to refer to. Otherwise, it

---

* I am just old enough to have used a telex machine in its last few fading years, at one of my first jobs. It was clumsy to use and always breaking down. The company I worked for distributed guides to hotels for business travelers. There actually was such a publication, physical, heavy, with glossy color photography; trees were dying for this thing, and slowly, so was I. Spiritually I quickly reached the point of Scarlett O'Hara wolfing down a turnip wrested in desperation from the hard ground and vowing never to be hungry again. I went to grad school.

is clothes without a body, just as emoticons alone would be. Neither decorations, detritus, nor destructors, emoticons are—you knew this was coming—the faces of texting.

Part of why emoticons seem like add-ons rather than mix-ins is that they are drawings rather than writing in the proper sense. However, their equivalent in speech is actual words that are, in their way, faces. This chapter has been an attempt to show how central such words are to language as it actually is. No known language has ever lacked FACE-ial words like the new *like*, the new *totally*, and the new *ass*. German has its *mal* and many more, without which one is not truly speaking the language. Ask your Japanese friend what *ne* means: from the smiles, hesitations, and shrugs in the answer, you'll know you're in FACE land. The classicist who knows her Ancient Greek can talk your ear off about that language's "particles" and how elusive their meanings are. Much of the problem is FACE fifth-century-Athens style: we don't have living speakers to teach us what the nuances actually were by using the "particles" in live context.

When hearing people who are fluent in American Sign Language have a conversation among themselves, often they will slide into using some signs with their speech. On describing a political address, they might mention the candidate talking while making the sign for *lying*, to indicate how likely it was that the candidate was telling the truth. *I moved to Los Angeles*, someone will say, making the sign for "put down roots" while saying *moved*, adding a nuance that in speech alone would be conveyed vaguely with intonation, if at all. This, like so much else, is the manifestation of feelings ever pushing out from behind mere statements.

That's what FACE is about. No language qualifies as a
real one without it. Much of what occasions questions as to
"What's *that* all about?" in how people come to use words
is ultimately a mere matter of language maintaining that
which it could never do without. A language without FACE
would be as discomfitingly incomplete as a human without
a face—just as we would expect, given that languages
express humanity.

2

It's the Implication That Matters

Words on the Move

You may know a data scientist. I don't, however, and if I met one at a party I'd need filling in on just what a data scientist is ("I shall take this data and *scient* it!").

And I would find out that the term refers to people whose function for a company is to use statistical knowledge to identify and illustrate trends in the Big Data mined by today's computing technology. My, my, though—the uses of *data* and *scientist* in the term *data scientist* are extremely specific, aren't they? Data is supposed to be facts; one must be taught that in *data scientist* the reference is to Big Data in particular. And the *scientist* part seems rather odder: isn't a scientist someone in a lab coat examining things, usually either liquid, tiny, or far off in the heavens? Certainly, statistics and computers fit under the science umbrella—but data *scientist*? Okay . . .

That term may seem like a bit of a stunt. Yet it represents a perfectly normal phenomenon: the meanings of words are ever on the move.

Shakespeare will help us get a better handle on this process and how eternal it is. We're at a performance of Shakespeare's *Henry V.* The grand old St. Crispin's Day speech is already past; now we're in Act V. Henry is visiting the French court; the Duke of Burgundy wants peace. Constant war is leaving everyone numb to the finer things that make life worth living:

> *And as our vineyards, fallows, meads, and hedges,*
> *Defective in their natures, grow to wildness,*
> *Even so our houses and ourselves and children*
> *Have lost, or do not learn for want of time,*
> *The sciences that should become our country,*
> *But grow like savages . . .*

No one ever said Shakespearean language was as easy to take in as the language of a sitcom, but all seems well enough so far. It may seem a little odd to say that we have lost our "sciences," given that Burgundy would seem to be interested in broader issues of cultural and psychological decline. However, it's pretty easy to wrap our heads around the idea that Burgundy might alight upon the issue of "science" in passing—as in, perhaps, technical knowledge (like using statistics to identify trends in Big Data?). Call it the "poetic" aspect of Shakespeare.

But then comes something that simply doesn't make sense, which we have to just let pass. Burgundy says that the purpose of this convocation is to "reduce" the state of things to what they were before ("Which to reduce into our former favor / You are assembled") such that peace will "expel these inconveniences / And bless us with her former qualities." But if going back to normal would be a "blessing," then why would it be a "reduction"?

In its modern meaning, *reduce* is simply incoherent in that passage. It implies that the change would be a minimization, something unwelcome. One might force a reading according to which the current barbarisms are in some way large, as an excrescence that needs "reducing" in the sense of a hedge grown astray. However, that reading is, indeed, forced—surely not one Shakespeare would have randomly tossed into something as finely wrought as a play like this one. More important, he sought to be understood, by people hearing the text delivered orally, at speed, once. So why did he write "reduced"?

Because the word had a different meaning in his time. You can glean what it would have been from how the word is composed: *re+duce*. The *duce* part is from the Latin word for "to lead," more familiar to us from the Italian descendant of that word *Il Duce*, "The Leader." *Reduce*, when first borrowed into English from French in the late fourteenth century, meant what its parts mean: to lead again. *Reduce* was essentially a fancier way of saying "go back," and that's what Shakespeare meant. "Reduce into our former favor" had nothing to do with diminution or descent; it meant, simply, to take things back to the way they used to be. Shakespeare was following in the tradition of ancient usages of the word, such as a religious call in a source from 1400 for people to "reduce me in to the right way" if "I have gone beside the way"—the "right" way being something one seeks to return to, not sink into the muck of. Even in 1664, some time after Shakespeare, a writer described the Romans after their colonization of Britain as having "reduced the natural Inhabitants from their Barbarism to the Society of civil Life," a passage that is senseless unless we understand that reducing was a matter of return, not destruction.

Only in the eighteenth century did *reduce* come to always mean what it does to us. It happened gradually, as a result of the fact that words' meanings always have certain redolences beyond what we consciously consider. If you take something back to the way it was, that process will typically involve either improvement or ruin of some degree. For transformation to result in something neither better nor worse is, perhaps, what we least expect. *Reduce*, then, would as often as not have meant not only return but betterment, as in the Shakespeare quote. But just as often, it would have meant not only return but lessening, and in Middle and Early Modern English, quotes illustrating that are just as common as ones illustrating improvement. They are more common, actually—such that as things panned out, *reduce* was used so often with an added implication of diminishment that after a while, diminishment was actually what the word was always used to mean.

By the eighteenth century, then, *reduce* had lost its old flexibility: you "reduced" something no longer to its former glory but to squalor. Before long, reduction was referring to liquids and even the act of dieting. "Dearie, I must tell you, I'm reducing!" the old-time society dowager would say in refusing that éclair—in response to which an Elizabethan would have said, "Reducing what, and back to where?"

Words Do Not Sit Still

In chapter 1, I focused on one possible pathway of change words can undergo, the shift from the neutral to the personal. However, that is only one of a great many pathways a word may drift down as time passes. The difference between our sense of what *reduce* means and Shakespeare's demonstrates something general about how language works. It isn't that a certain curiosity cabinet of a few dozen words happened to have different meanings hundreds of years ago. Just about all words in any language have different meanings now than they did in the past. Some words' meanings hold on longer than others. Some few even hold on to the same meaning for thousands of years. However, it is they, and not the *reduce*s, that are the oddities, mostly a homely collection of especially heavily used words, living fossils analogous to horseshoe crabs and coelacanths. The word *brother*, for example, has meant the same thing for at least seven thousand or so years (and probably longer), ever since the language that later became most of Europe's languages was still a tribal one spoken in the south of what is now Ukraine. (Linguists call it Proto-Indo-European.) Or, the word for *I* traces back with the same meaning that far and likely farther, although its sounds have changed so much that many will not feel that it has remained "the same word." (It was probably *eg* in ancient Ukraine.) But beyond a few words like these, change is the default; it's stasis that is weird. By *science*, for example, the Duke of Burgundy in *Henry V* (like Shakespearean characters in general) meant "knowledge." Only later did the word come to refer only to knowledge having to do with the systematic understanding of the natural world.

The change happens slowly, step by step. Consider that in terms of what *in-* and *numerable* mean, *innumerable* "should" refer to something that cannot be counted for some reason. And that's just how it started, as in a writer in 1485 exclaiming that the amount of his love for someone is "innumerable to express." That meant that the amount can't be numerated—the writer even spelled it "In-nvmerabyll," complete with the hyphen. (Can we even pretend that this spelling, despite that people then hardly intended such orthography as "cute," doesn't make the proclamation seem more sincere?)

But even this early, you can smell the *implication* hanging over things. If something can't be counted, it just *might* be because it's covered with mud, and it just *might* be because you're too far away, but more likely, the reason something resists counting is because there is a great amount of it. To be innumerable is probably, in life as we know it, to be a lot. After a while, that implication affected the meaning of the word so consistently that new generations thought of the "a lot" component of the meaning as part of the meaning itself rather than a mere redolence. Soon, one could no longer use *innumerable* to refer to something unable to be counted for some other reason. Today, if the reason you can't count the rats under the floorboards happens to be because you can't see them, you just *might* declare the rats "innumerable" and stand by that forced usage of the word. However, you'd be about as misunderstood as the dowager telling the Elizabethan that she's "reducing."

Step by step, the degree of the transformation can be rather gorgeous. In Old English the word *sælig* meant "blessed." Today, we're still using that word—it's our *silly*—but in what would seem to be a quite unrelated meaning. And it is, unless you imagine the step-by-step inching along that words do. If you're blessed, it stands to reason that you're innocent. If you're innocent, it stands to reason that in having been accused of the opposite, you've been someone in the down position—and probably in some way still are, even though you are now exonerated. If you're in the down position, it may not stand to reason per se that you're feeble in some way, but the suspicion hardly seems utterly unwarranted. Then, if you're feeble, it isn't completely counterintuitive to associate the feebleness with degree of mental acuity, upon which one might be assailed as weak-minded: i.e., a silly-billy. There's how our word for being a goofball began as one whose soundtrack would have been an "Amen" chord.

It's like the litter box, at least in my life. Back in the day, both my wife and I changed it. Then, when she first got pregnant, she stopped doing it because it's considered unhealthy for pregnant women to do the job. (Something about some virus?) So, I was always the one to change the box; it became "my job," such that my doing it became the norm. After the pregnancy, that norm stuck via inertia—the fact that no one really enjoys doing it discouraged my wife from taking it back up, and the fact that it's a light task discouraged me from bothering to say anything about it. But this means that today when our daughters see my wife occasionally doing it when I am away, they find it peculiar. "Mommy, why are *you* changing the kitty litter?" I suspect that to them, changing the cat box is a gendered activity, or possibly one connected specifically only to me.

None of this has anything to do with the structure and function of the box, of course. Chance factors presented my daughters with a perception that has become, for them, a reality. Our reality is what we experience; history is lore while the future is speculation. In the same way, our sense of what *reduce* and *innumerable* mean is the result of chance conventions in their usage having edged out what the words originally meant to create new realities of usage. Crucially, even what the words meant before is not what they had meant before that—this kind of change is eternal. The *-numer-* part of *innumerable* comes out elsewhere as *number*, which was once a word that meant to mete out. You can imagine how that meaning could drift into the concept of amount. It did.

In this chapter we will go beyond the one type of change we saw in chapter 1, and embrace the word in general as a fundamentally impermanent association of a sequence of sounds with a particular meaning. The concept in itself is hardly unfamiliar. Scholars of not only linguistics but philosophy, anthropology, and beyond are familiar with the pioneer linguist Ferdinand de Saussure's conception of the arbitrariness of the sign in relation to what it refers to. There is nothing inherently canine about the word *dog*, which is clear from the fact that the word differs so much from language to language.

Less often aired, however, is that this arbitrariness allows words' meanings to change constantly. One sequence of sounds is as useful to mean one thing as another, as long as some other sequence of sounds comes in to replace the earlier meaning. English speakers first referred to dogs as *hounds*; *dog* came in later. The sequences of sounds are eternally slipping around the field of meanings that a language must cover. At any one time, everything necessary is expressible via the particular web of linkages between sound sequences and meanings that exists at that time. But by the time anyone has compiled a dictionary of any one stage in these linkages, it is already somewhat obsolete, because the language, as a conglomeration of inherently temporary linkages between form and meaning, has already moved along.

Note that this means that this chapter is about neither a problem nor a mystery. The lesson is not that words' meanings are so unclear and subjective that true communication is grievously difficult. It can be, but not because of the fluidity of word-meaning combinations that, at any given time, afford perfectly efficient communication, of the kind we engage in daily. This chapter is about peace. When we understand that language has always been, always will be, and could function as nothing else but a system of self-regulating instability, language sounds better.

Auditions, Commodities, and Minorities:
Some Examples

Those fond of books on language may be familiar with one facet of the inherent changeability of words' meanings. It is traditionally covered that meanings have either broadened or narrowed over time. This indeed happens. To return to *dog*, for instance, when *hound* was the normal word for a canine, *dog* was a word for a big, fierce sort of dog, it seems. Over time, it came to be used as the all-purpose word for *dog*. That was a classic case of semantic broadening, paralleled by the narrowing of the scope of *hound*, which now refers only to a dog used for hunting. (Chihuahuas aren't hounds.)

Many words have narrowed under the radar, in certain usages. "Does he drink?" is a question about alcohol, not whether the person imbibes liquids in general. In the old days (roughly the first half of the twentieth century) the question "Do you like music?" referred to classical music; no one questioned whether a person enjoyed a pop tune, a jig, or a lullaby. That assumption that "music" refers to classical is now antique, but lives on in how readily a textbook, or even a trade book, on classical music can be titled as about "music," as if Brahms and Schoenberg are somehow the default conception of music, with rock, jazz, hip-hop, Peruvian *huayno* music, and Indian ragas somehow not "*music* music." More subtly, today discussions about the value of "reading" presuppose that the topic is fiction: "reading" is not assumed to include books about the Thirty

Years' War, the cosmos, or cod. In this vein, "language" in the conception of most people brings the printed word to mind first, with speech considered an afterthought. Hence questions such as "What is texting doing to language?" despite the fact that it would be impossible to speak with capital letters or to utter a sequence of emoticons.

However, broadening and narrowing alone do not convey the essence of the matter. Alone, they imply that words' meanings change in a clear direction, which feels intuitive, only minorly transformative. *Meat*, say, was first used to refer to all food (hence candy being called sweet-meat) but narrowed to refer to flesh. This change was pretty cozy as change goes—all within one realm of things, food. Yet the more common reality is plain old drift, along the lines of the pathway from *blessed* to *silly*, where the issue is less broadening or narrowing than simply transformation. Broadening and narrowing happen, but a more general characterization of words over time is that they have a way of just oozing around. *Bird* is an example. It started as a word meaning a baby animal, but later became the word for flying animals. That's a lateral shift—neither more nor less specific, just different. (The old word for flying animal was *fugol*, which narrowed into today's *fowl*, referring to certain barnyard birds and ones like them.) A word we utter is usually just the latest stage in tens of millennia of drifting from one meaning into another.

Here are five examples, of merry morphings from points quite distant, that nevertheless seem so eternal, as if they had never been anything but themselves.

Let's start with a seemingly ordinary word like *audition*. Shouldn't it mean "hearing" in terms of what we otherwise expect of the *aud-* root? *Audio* comes to mind, as well as *audiovisual, audiology,* etc. Yet *audition* immediately brings to mind someone trying out for a part in a play or film. That's only because of implication and drift.

When it first appeared in English, borrowed from Latin, *audition* indeed meant "hearing." When a doctor recommended a substance that "draweth all out which is in the Eares, and administreth good auditione," he meant that having your ears clear of whatever the disgusting stuff was, your hearing got better, not that it got you a part in the latest production of *Henry V*.

However, naturally, tryouts for such productions might naturally come to be called "hearings," as they involved listening to someone recite. If one wanted to fancy up the word "hearing" a bit, a tendency hardly unlikely among writerly sorts, then the term would be *audition*. To people in the late nineteenth century who first started using *audition* in that way, the word would have meant what it sounded like; the component of hearing in the word would have been intuitively felt. In fact, the word was first used for musical tryouts, where sound was indeed all that mattered, as opposed to appearance and movement.

However, after a while, *audition* came to be used solely in reference to tryouts for performances, while elsewhere, *hearing* became the word English speakers beyond medical practitioners used to refer to the perception of sound. Then implication settled in: if it's an audition when someone gets up and sings, then it hardly seems unreasonable to call it an audition as well when the next person gets up and does an acrobatic trick. Today, one could audition to be a mime. To an Elizabethan, that usage would sound as strange as doing tai chi to get a part in *La Bohème*.

I have written that words' changes in meaning create no ambiguity, but I can be accused of having overstated the matter somewhat: if there is an area of English in which language change has truly hindered understanding for many, it is financial terms. As John Lanchester has put it:

> "Credit" has been reversified: it means debt. "Inflation" means money being worth less. "Synergy" means sacking people. "Risk" means precise mathematical assessment of probability. "Noncore assets" means garbage.

And there is so much more. Take *commodity* (please!). We are accustomed to hearing the term used to refer to certain staple products whose quality is largely invariant no matter the producer, such as salt and crude oil. More precisely, commodities are associated with futures contracts offered to producers of them, which guarantee a uniform price regardless of fluctuations in the market—good for the seller when the market is down, and for the contract holder when the market is up. That is an almost viciously specific usage for a term that even people outside finance are regularly confronted with. However, the temptation to blame financiers for wanting to keep their business obscure is unnecessary. What has happened to *commodity* is the same thing that happened to *sælig* (as well as to my wife cleaning the litter box).

Commodity was first a word about comfort, as in *accommodation*. A 1488 book printed by the pioneer printer of English William Caxton dismisses certain men who excessively "encline to the rest and commodity of the body." Anyone would spontaneously extend that meaning to things that *make* one comfortable and are therefore, in themselves, commodities. Thus by 1615 there were usages such as describing the god Vulcan as "the first that found out the commodity of fire." Fire would have been as novel and invaluable a comfort, i.e., a commodity, to earlier man as eye pillows and Jack Daniel's are to us now.

But from there, it's a short step to thinking of a whole class of staple items as basic commodities of life, such that the word that began as describing the pleasure of spreading out on a sofa was now applied to soybeans heaped cold and dirty in a freight car in January. All that's needed to get from there to now is the incorporation of products like that into a futures market, such that commodities are discussed less in and of themselves than as a shorthand for futures contracts based on them that yield an abstract form of recompense. From stretching out after a long day to a soybean to an intangible and vaguely seedy financial arrangement—step by step.

Fine comes from the French word *fin*, which means end. Even in French the word had morphed—one way of being at the end of something is to be at the top of the line, the ultimate, the best. Think of the quaintish expression "the living end" to praise something. Hence *fin* meant both "end" as well as "of high quality," and the latter meaning is what made it into English. "Men findis lompis on the sand Of ter, nan finer in that land," says the historical chronicle *Cursor Mundi* around 1300—"You find lumps on the sand of tar, none finer in that land." Tar? I know; tastes vary, but we can accept that if one were into tar, certain lumps of it could qualify as fine indeed—as in solid, lovely, and exquisite. (I'm trying!) In any case, we still use *fine* that way in *a fine day* or *a fine rendition*.

However, notice that those usages are a touch quaint in feel, and meanwhile, the word has moved along elsewhere. People today also associate *fine* with the meaning "delicate"—fine lace, fine distinctions. That is based on implication: one way for something to be of high quality is to be made with delicate precision. If things of that nature are referred to as fine with enough frequency, people will start to link the word not just to high quality, but to more specific things like delicate tracery, doily patterns, just the right violin, dainty walks, and so on.

Meanwhile, those who would not think of the "delicate" meaning might mention the usage "I'm fine" in response to being asked how one is doing. Here, the meaning is neither "exquisite" as a lump of tar nor "delicate" like lace, but a wan assurance that one is unhurt. ("Oh, I'm fine—it was just a scratch.") Emotional and social expressions have a way of watering down with use. *Good-bye* started as "God be with you," *darn* started as "eternal damnation," *LOL* started as "laughing out loud." *I'm fine* began as meaning one was terrific, with that earlier meaning of *fine* (in the sense that requires us today to say we are "great" or "fantastic"), but gradually whittled down with centuries of use into meaning "I'm not dead."

Thus the answer to "What does *fine* mean?" is richer than we might suppose, because words don't sit still. The word we see at the end of a French film meaning "end"— *FIN*—in English has a different meaning before a noun (*a fine day*) than after it (*My father is fine*), and elsewhere refers to the texture of a hairnet. Then, let's not even get into the *fine* that you can be given for parking in the wrong place, which is, indeed, another drifting from that same word that once just meant "end."

Minority in American English has taken on, via implications, a meaning quite far from what the word originally referred to. One may even never have occasion to consider that *minority*'s "real" meaning is supposed to be "the smaller portion." What began as a technical and euphemistic reference to people of color was used in that way so often that today, in the minds of American English speakers *minority* refers specifically to people of the color in question: brown. That is, minorities are considered to be black and Latino people. *Minority* feels forced when applied to other groups, even when they, too, constitute numerical minorities of the population. The word has often felt somewhat awkward applied even to Asians, and when whites technically become a numerical minority in the United States, *minority* will likely not be transferred to them.

Rather, to the extent that the term survives, it will likely continue to be applied to black and Latino people, especially in more casual conversations even when Latinos outnumber whites. "We're all minorities now!" some will point out—upon which most will guiltily feel that the word doesn't feel right when applied to whites. That feeling will be justified, since in its demographic usage, *minority* ceased to be a numerical term sometime in the seventies, whatever the dictionary definition specifies. Word meanings drift as always, this time from referring to a proportion to referring to dark-complected people. "He's a minority"—imagine how queerly illogical that sentence would sound to someone transported to our times from 1600. "A minority of what?"

Merry started out meaning "short," believe it or not. But that which is short is often pleasant, since so many things go on too long. Note how *pastime* (as in passing the time), for example, connotes the joys of brevity contravened by *Die Walküre* and *Apocalypse Now*. After a while, a word that first meant "short" meant "short and sweet" and finally, just "sweet." Meanwhile, earlier English did have the word *short* itself, but even that word had once meant something different: "sliced off." That which results from cutting off is often a short thing, hence . . .

The joyous meaning of *merry* was a beautiful demonstration of the element of chance in how words' meanings move along. The earliest rendition we can get a sense of for *merry* is that on the Ukrainian steppes several thousand years ago, in Proto-Indo-European, it was *mregh*. In Greece, this word for "short" morphed not into merriment but into the word for upper arm, *brakhion*. The sounds in *mregh* and *brakh* match better than it looks on paper: for one thing, both *m* and *b* are produced by putting your lips together, and so it's easy for one to change into the other. As to meaning, it was a matter of implications, this time in one of the things the word was applied to rather than the word itself. The upper arm is shorter than the lower, and hence one might start referring to the upper arm as the "shorter," and the rest was history. Calling your upper arm your "shorter" is not appreciably odder than calling cutoff pants shorts, after all.

The process never stops. It seems that in Latin this *brakh* ended up, among other places, in a pastry, namely, one resembling folded arms, called a *brachitella*. Old High German picked that up as *brezitella*; by Middle High German people were saying *brezel*. Today, *brezel* is *pretzel*—from that same word that meant short and now connotes joyousness in English. In France, that *brach* root drifted into a word referring to shoulder straps or, by extension, a child's little chemise undershirt. Women can wear chemises, too, but garments, like words, have a way of changing over the centuries, and after a while the *brassière* had evolved into a more specific anatomical dedication than a chemise's. The modern word *bra*, then, is what happens when a word for "short" drifts step by step into new realms. *Merry, pretzel,* and *bra* are, in a sense, all the same word—yet contests could be held challenging people to even use all three in a sentence (or at least one that made any sense).

More How Than Why: The Role of Chance

But *why?*

Fine starts as a word for "the end," but drifts into meaning "delicate" here, "unhurt" there, and even "a payment required in penalty" elsewhere. Why those meanings and not others? After all, couldn't *audition* have come to refer to something you hear in your imagination, since *vision* can refer to a mirage or a hallucination? Why couldn't *merry* have gone from meaning "short" to meaning "of little consequence" and then, via implication, perhaps "contemptible"? Why couldn't it have been *actually* instead of *really* that became a factuality marker we sprinkle throughout our sentences? We say *I'm sick of this weather, really.* But wouldn't *I'm sick of this weather, actually* have been fine, too? One seeks rules.

But in the end, we have to be satisfied with understanding the "how." There is an element of chance in how language changes, such that to an extent, the process must be approached as a kind of spectator sport. There are odds to be discussed—*weep* isn't going to jump into meaning "fingernail"—but overall, you can't know just what's going to happen going in.

The process is channeled by intuitive metaphorical variations on what a word means: *weep,* for example, started as meaning "yell"—it's easy to see how one gets from yelling to crying. However, the *particular* direction a word happens to take is subject to explanation after the fact but not prediction before it. Romance languages like French get their word for *weep* from a word that once meant "to beat the chest," which is no less understandable than getting it from *yell*, or than the fact that the word for *yell* that became *weep* in English ended up meaning to get a beating over in Italy in Latin. Again, explicable—but hardly what one would *predict* out of other potential possibilities.

Yet our natural inclination is to seek causes, with a sense that the only complete account of a metamorphosis is one where all is not only described, but explained. Chance feels, indeed, random. Explanations based on chance seem antithetical to the scientific enterprise itself, seeming to suggest we haven't tried hard enough. Yet while a science worth pursuing cannot rely excessively on chance, chance is baked into a great many transformational processes, such that to refuse the role of randomness is to not truly understand them.

Example: we are taught that natural selection favors mutations that increase an organism's chances for survival. However, fin whales' lower jaws are white on the right side and mottled black on the left, while their tongues are colored the opposite way. This quirk clearly offers the animal no survival advantage. ("Mmm, I want me some of *that*! Makes him look stronger.") It is a genetic accident carried down generations because it does no harm. In popular music, the fade-out ending had a long vogue. It fell out of favor, and a search for a reason leads nowhere. Nothing about modern American culture is any less compatible with a fade-out ending than it was forty years ago.

In the same way, chance is one of the keystones of language change. For example, *awesome* is a compliment, *awful* is a put-down. Yet there isn't anything inherently positive about the ending *-some*, as we know from *loathsome* and *gruesome*. Nor is *-ful* inherently negative—note *wonderful* and *bountiful*. *Awesome* is good and *awful* is bad solely because of how the cookie happened to crumble, as we know from the fact that *awful* actually used to be a compliment as well. Shakespeare is always use*ful* in such cases, as when the Duke of York condemns the king in *Henry VI, Part 2*:

> *That head of thine doth not become a crowne*
> *Thy hand is made to grasp a palmer's staff*
> *And not to grace an awefull Princely Sceptre.*

Here is another one of those moments where taking Shakespeare according to the modern meaning of the words trips us up. If Henry is so unfit for authority, then why is York describing the scepter as "awful"? Doesn't he mean "awesome"? He did—except that's what *awful* meant in his time. In 1660 a history of science purrs of an "awful Silence on the shady Hills," where *awful* is again meant positively. One could use *awful* that way into the 1800s, and even today, when we say *awfully good*, we mean it as a compliment. Otherwise, after that, *awesome* began to take over in the positive role, while *awful* went sour.*

---

* Some will be waiting for the tale of Charles II praising St. Paul's Cathedral as "awful, pompous and artificial," with the lesson being that those words' meanings have all gone from negative to positive. Believe me, I'd

There was no more reason for that than that there is a difference between *entrance* and *entry*. The native English speaker knows that one blocks an *entrance* while one manages *entry* into a place, that one suffers through a job involving data *entry*, not data *entrance*. Think also of *status* versus *station*. Both words are children of the same Latin root and started as meaning "standing." We most associate *status* with that meaning today, but in an alternate universe, *station* could do the job as well, which we know because it actually did in the past. We can tell today from the antique expression *rank and station*, one of those deliberately redundant expressions like *hale and hearty*, where *station* meant what *rank* did. But we encounter the living usage more than we might think, in the Declaration of Independence:

> . . . it becomes necessary for one people to dissolve the political bands which have connected them with one another, and to assume among the powers of the earth, the separate and equal *station* to which the Laws of Nature and of Nature's God entitle them . . . .

We may be used to the *station* in this text, but if we pause to truly drink in the meaning of this sentence word by word, *station* is a bit of toe stubbing. One may read past it as

---

have used it, but the anecdote is actually one of those Game-of-Telephone distortions where a morsel becomes a meal. All the king said was "artificial," although that was, indeed, a compliment then, not having taken on its negative meaning via *implications* about that which is not natural.

something fancy—"poetic," perhaps. But Thomas Jefferson wasn't seeking poesy, of course: this document was intended as a precise, flinty proclamation. The sentence reads with perfect clarity if we substitute *status* for *station*: the idea is that nations have separate and equal status. This is the term that translations of the document into other languages use, for example. *Station* here isn't poetic or "high"—it was a conventional way of expressing the concept; *rank and station* didn't sound quaint to people speaking English then. *Status* became the established replacement for *station* in this usage only in the nineteenth century. But it wasn't that *station* was somehow insufficient; things just drifted. *Awesome* and *awful, station* and *status.*

Or *um* and *uh.* Pausing, one might say *uh* and one might say *um.* In our times, across America *um* is becoming more common than *uh.* Why it's *um* rather than *uh* taking over is something no one could furnish an explanation for even at gunpoint. Is it that there is something quietly off-putting about the sound *uh*? Apparently not, given something else that happened in the language not long ago. In literature of the early twentieth century and before, a locution that always reads a little weirdly is people saying *hey* where we now say *huh.* From F. Scott Fitzgerald's short story "May Day" in 1920:

> "Beautiful morning," he said gravely, squinting up his owlish eyes.
> "Probably is."
> "Go get some breakfast, hey?"
> Dean agreed, with additions. "Breakfast and liquor."

Today, that'd be "Go get some breakfast, huh?" just as today, the tramp who growls "Tryin' to kid me, hey?" in Fitzgerald's "A Luckless Santa Claus" in 1912 would say "Tryin' to kid me, huh?" (although *kid* would likely not be the word of choice). This is by no means a Fitzgerald quirk: this *hey* is common in fiction and comic strips of the period. It's just that *huh* (with the same sound as *uh*) gradually eased this *hey* out. So *um* bests *uh* today, while not too long ago practically the same sound, *huh*, bested *hey*.

The best name for things like this is flutter. Words in a language are always oozing here and there over time. A language has a grid of meanings that includes everything human beings need to say: animal, dribble, maybe, already, quick, above, stupid, Hey!, gristle, without, suppose, take out of, slither into—tens of thousands of meanings at the very least. A language needs this grid of meanings expressed by words—that is, packets of sounds. However, it doesn't matter which packets of sounds cover which meanings, as long as speakers know which packets happen to be covering which meanings at the time. And that's a good thing, because the inevitability of looming implications keeps inching the packets of sounds into new directions. The words are, together, like a soft film sliding slowly around upon the grid of meanings.

This reality requires visualization. Let's say that in any language, there are the basic concepts of food, meat, bread, vegetables, fruit, crumbs, and nourishment in the abstract sense of what we often express as "fuel." Here is a grid of all those meanings, represented by pictures to reinforce that these are not words but what the words refer to.

In Old English, the packets of sounds linked to those meanings were different from what we are familiar with today. For purposes of clarity, the words are translated into their modern renditions:

Food

Meat

Bread

Loaf

Wort

Apple

Meat was the word for what we would today express as *food*, a word for which existed but had the more abstract meaning of "nourishment." What we call *meat* or *flesh* was called *flesh*.* The word *bread* was used for pieces, bits and crumbs of food in general; what we call *bread* was called *loaf*. Vegetables

---

* I am oversimplifying slightly, in that the *flesh* word was used more, at least in the Old English documents that survive, to refer to flesh in contrast with the soul. What we know as meat was more often referred to as "fleshmeat."

were called *wort*, the rather marginal word we now use only for certain medicinal herbs. *Apple* was a generic word for fruit.

Fast-forward to now, and the words have shifted around. We can express all the same concepts; what has changed is which packets of sounds we link to them. *Food* has edged out *meat* as the generic term for "eats"; *meat* has moved into the slot once reserved for *flesh*. What Old English speakers called *loaf* we now call *bread*, while *loaf* refers to a single table's serving of said bread. A word *crumb* meaning "fragment"

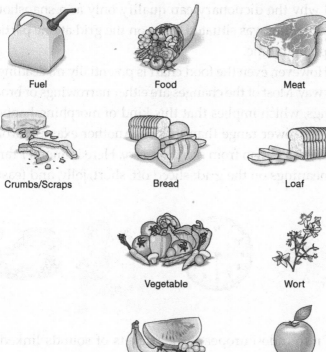

Fuel	Food	Meat
Crumbs/Scraps	Bread	Loaf

Vegetable	Wort

Fruit	Apple

now occupies the slot *bread* once did. New words can also come from other languages: *vegetable* and *fruit* came in from French, so often the source of words for more formal things such as delicacies of the table. That edged *wort* out into its modern health food store reference, while *apple* came to refer to that certain red fruit that is never quite as good as you wish it would be. *Nourishment*, too, is from French. Meanwhile, we have *fuel* and *nourishment* to express what *food* once did.

Picture this process happening across tens of thousands of words all the time. That is the essence of what words are, and why the dictionary can qualify only as a snapshot of how the film was situated upon on the grid at one particular point in time.

However, even the food chart is potentially misleading in one way. Most of the changes are either narrowings or broadenings, which implies that this kind of morphing happens in a narrower range than it does. Another example would be that transition from *short* to *merry*. Here is another range of meanings on the grid: sliced off, short, jolly, and feast:

In Proto-Indo-European, the packets of sounds linked to those concepts were quite unlike what we would expect. The words given are the English descendants of the words, rather than the Proto-Indo-European words themselves—a chart with the likes of *mregh* on it would look less informative than soiled:

Short   Merry   Festive

The word we know as *short* was used to mean "cut or sliced off." One word for *short* was what we today know in English as *merry*. Meanwhile, a word to express what we know as *merry*, i.e., "jolly," was one that we know especially in the word *festive*.

But in English, the place of those packets of sound has shifted around. If something is sliced off, chances are that it is not long—hence, that word can come to mean "short," and that's where English's *short* comes from. (In Latin the same process yielded a word it later gave us, *curt*, in which that sense of cutting is still perceptible.) For *cut off*, we have, well, *cut off*. The *merry* word, as we have seen, came to mean "jolly." *Festive* has not been ousted from the "jolly" slot, but it is a rather starchy word, almost canceling out the atmosphere of what it is supposed to refer to, and rarely used by most. However, that same root is still used in a more ordinary way in the form of *feast*.

These illustrations are, of course, highly schematized. In reality, words do not shift from one meaning to another

| Cut Off | Short | Merry | (Festive) Feast |

abruptly—for a good while they retain elements of both meanings. For a period, *reduce* was used mainly for minimization but could still be used for aggrandizement as well. Even now, *fine* means "delicate" and "okay" while the original "excellent" meaning holds on as well, with a guess being that only in some future stage of English will the "excellent" meaning, already less robust than the others, wear away into true archaism. However, the main lesson is the eternally, inevitably slippery relationship between the film of words and the grid of meanings. Words are not handed down on tablets and locked into place; they are squirted out of a tube to float around.

One might wonder how words can be useful if their meanings are so inherently unstable. That fear is much of why so many are irritated to see such changes in meaning; one envisions people groping for mutual comprehension. However, this will never happen: as unpredictable as words' driftings are, they drift according to a subconscious communality. The implications that pull a word's meaning in a new direction are ones that all speakers intuit, not the idiosyncratic fancies of single persons ("Rain reminds me of *using a fork!*"). To associate innocence with a lack of power is natural of human cognition; hence *silly* passed through those two meanings, not "spicy" or "rough to the touch."

Language is for communicating, and this simple fact bars words' drifting in an incoherent way that would impede understanding. Chapter 1 showed how readily words drift into tools for reinforcing and marking various shades of interpersonal understanding. That same impulse channels words' changes of meaning into mentally processible directions, allowing a language to maintain its basic function.

Changes in meaning are as natural to words as changes of pitch are to music. When a note stays unchanged for an eternity, it's unexpected, suggesting either plainchant, willful modernist contrarianism, or bagpipes. Few consider any of those three the essence of what music is, and when we expect words to change just as we expect notes to change, an advantage is that English language looks different in the past, present, and future.

In the Past: The "Poetry" of Shakespeare

To truly know that a word is a thing ever in flux can help us understand the language of the past—or why the language of the past can be so hard to fully understand. Shakespeare is, again, a useful demonstration: *reduce* is hardly alone in his work in throwing the modern listener or reader. Have you ever attended a Shakespeare play and kept to yourself, as everyone around you was exclaiming about how wonderful it was, that you missed so much of what any of the characters were saying that you'd be hard-pressed to say you took in the plot in any detail? My sense over the years has been that asking people about this creates precisely the same discomfort as asking if they floss every night.

Commonly we are told that Shakespeare's language is "high," such that the challenge can be met by making a certain effort. Related to this is the idea that Shakespeare's language is poetic, requiring more effort to process than the phraseology of Neil Simon. Then someone will say that the language comes across best with careful acting technique, ideally wielded by British people.

All claims except the one about Brits are true. However, many will be nagged by a feeling that there is more to the story, and there is. When, in *Hamlet*, Polonius opens his farewell speech to Laertes ("Neither a borrower nor a lender be") with "And these few precepts in thy memory / See thou character," rising to a challenge can take us only so far. We can indeed process *precepts*, *thy*, and *thou* with the aforesaid rising. But what does Polonius mean by *character*? Neither intonation, facial expression, being British, nor rising will get across that in Shakespeare's time that word meant "write," as in the characters that one writes. Polonius is telling Laertes, in short, "Note these things well."

At the very start of *Measure for Measure*, Duke Vincentio announces:

> *Of government the properties to unfold,*
> *Would seem in me to affect speech and discourse;*
> *Since I am put to know that your own science,*
> *Exceeds, in that, the lists of all advice*
> *My strength can give you; then no more remains ...*

The reason we could grasp almost no meaning from this when spoken in real time, and might get little more even reading it on the page, is not that the language is poetic. There isn't a Wordsworthian word in the passage. Yet one "rises" to this only to bump one's head. The problem is that so many of the words no longer mean what they did four hundred years ago.

And that is exactly what we would expect. Shakespearean text looks and sounds like the language we speak. Skim a text and usually no word leaps out as utterly unexpected. This is much of why we are told the task is simply to buck up. However, lurking behind the familiarity are many "false friends," of the kind students are warned about in learning French. *Sensible* means "sensitive" in French rather than "levelheaded." ("Sensible" is *sensé*.) If you hear or read *sensible* in French thinking it refers to common sense, you've missed something basic without even knowing it. In the same way, in the *Measure for Measure* passage, *affect* for Shakespeare meant "to make a pretense of," while *science* meant "knowledge." Thrown by both those when hearing this in real time, not to mention the now unconventional use of *unfold* in reference to speaking, we end up lost. Not because we are uncultured or incapable of effort, but because language is always moving. It's done a lot of that since 1600.

Another example is Edmund's cocky speech about his origins in *King Lear*:

> Wherefore should I
> Stand in the plague of custom and permit

> The curiosity of nations to deprive me
> For that I am some twelve or fourteen moonshines
> Lag of a brother?

To know that *wherefore* meant "why" is hardly a stretch, and we can likely agree that *moonshines* for "months" is poetic. All "rise"! However, why *curiosity*? With our poetic hats on we are poised to interpret it as meaning "something peculiar," but that meaning makes no sense here. "The curiosity of nations" can't mean that nations are a peculiar concept, since they aren't. But if *curiosity* more immediately reminds us of a healthy interest in matters outside oneself, then why is Edmund implying that curiosity is a bad thing?

Because in Shakespeare's time, *curiosity* meant "care" in the sense of close attention. In 1664 someone we would now call a scientist wrote about the resolution power of lenses, exclaiming that if the state of the art in his time "could attain to that curiosity as to grind us such Glasses . . . we might hazard at last the discovery of Spiritualities themselves." But was this man implying that astronomers of the time simply lacked sufficient interest in their own subject to bother to fashion more powerful lenses? It's weird little things like this that make antique prose so often seem a tad off, as if people then were incapable of expressing themselves quite as lucidly as we do. Actually, though, this writer was quite lucid: if we read *curiosity* in the passage as meaning "carefulness" or "precision," then all is clear.

By *curiosity*, then, Edmund means "fine distinctions," such as the kind that would label him as inferior for not being the eldest brother. To make such distinctions implies a certain interest, and over time that interest became the core meaning of the word itself, such that today we associate curiosity with schoolchildren, museums, and cats. However, in our times, the word has morphed into connoting not just interest, but something more specific: the positive kind of interest. Before things had gone that far, however, the curious person's interest could also be of a less welcome kind: in 1680 a bishop mentioned that "the opposition of Hereticks anciently occasioned too much Curiosity among the fathers." This is the flavor in Edmund's use of *curious*, and the issue is less poetry than the mere passage of time and its effects on arbitrary linkages between word and meaning.

Edmund continues:

> Why "bastard"? Wherefore "base"?
> When my dimensions are as well compact,
> My mind as generous, and my shape as true
> As honest madam's issue?

That all sounds like the language we speak, but in modern English it's actually a downright inept passage, not "poetry" at all. How does it refute an accusation of being lowly to assert that one's physique is modest and tidy—i.e., what *compact* most readily means to us? Also, if someone calls you illegitimate of birth, then isn't it a rather diagonal smackdown to mention that you are "generous"? There isn't anything poetic about that; in a modern playwright's script, that wouldn't make it past the first read-through. And most certainly, when called a bastard, no one venturing flinty self-assertion does themselves a favor by recounting their birth from a madam!

It's just that words move. *Compact* to Shakespeare meant "constructed." By implication, something well constructed is packed well, set nice and tight, and something with that quality often takes up less space than it could otherwise. Those realities have ooched *compact* away from what someone four hundred years ago could have imagined. *Generous*, meanwhile, meant noble, of all things. This explains why Edmund would note his mind as "generous" in response to being dismissed as low-class. In a 1607 "historie of four-footed beastes,"* on said beastes, the author decries that which "weakeneth their bodies, and dulleth in them all generosity," which clearly couldn't have meant that the animals were less likely to donate to charity. *Generosity* here meant noble quality, majesty. To the extent that nobility was associated with providing for a community, or at least having the wherewithal to do so, our modern sense of *generous* was a later development, via implication from the one that Shakespeare meant. And *madam*, of course, could still refer to women outside the oldest profession, as we see in the term of address "Madam" holding on by a thread today.

"If this letter speed / and my invention thrive, Edmund the base / shall top th' legitimate!"—definitely one can get used to *speed* meaning "to hurry," as we can still use the

---

* Note that even *history* meant something different in 1607: it still meant only "story" in a general sense, rather than specifically a disinterested recounting of past events. After all, in 1607, centuries before Wallace and Darwin, who knew that animals had a "history" in our sense?

word that way. But then comes another one of those patches of incomprehension that we are taught to consider lapses in our poetic sensibility*: *invention*. Edmund hasn't mentioned fashioning a lightbulb or a steam engine. By *invention*, he meant "plan." It makes sense: for *invention* to refer only to handy objects created in the basement and registered for patent is actually quite a narrowing of what *invention* could mean, and in fact once did mean. Drift happens—the words were at different places when Shakespeare was writing.

Way back in 1898, the Shakespearean scholar Mark H. Liddell argued in the *Atlantic Monthly* that these false friends in Shakespeare were such an impediment to understanding his language delivered live that it was time to include instruction in Elizabethan English in America's national secondary school curriculum. Of course, given the dazzling array of problems with public education in America, few could be under any impression that this could ever happen today or in any kind of foreseeable future. As such, others have argued that after four hundred years, because of normal processes of change, Shakespeare's language has become different enough from ours that the time has come to offer new versions of the plays translated into today's English.

Yes, I have been one of those people, and have experienced resistance (and even dribbles of vitriol) in response. However, most of this resistance has been based on the idea that the difference between our language and Shakespeare's

---

* Note that *sensibility* harbors the "sensitive" meaning as it does in French, while *sensible* itself drifted into a different meaning.

is only one of poetry, density, or elevation. The reason
Shakespeare's prose sounds so "poetic" is partly because it
is. But it is also partly for the more mundane reason that his
language is now, to a larger extent than we might prefer to
know, inaccessible to us without careful study on the page.

Many assume that the translation I refer to would have
to be into slang. I suspect this is because it can be so hard to
perceive that the very meanings of even the most mundane
of words have often changed so much—if one thinks the
difficulty of the language is merely a matter of "poetry,"
then it's easy to think that no translation in neutral current
English could be at issue, and hence the notion of "Yo,
whaddup, Calpurnia?" as a serious literary suggestion.

But I, for one, intend no such thing. The translations
could easily be better termed adjustments. Here is Macbeth
planning to kill Duncan:

Besides, this Duncan
Hath borne his faculties so meek, hath been
So clear in his great office, that his virtues
Will plead like angels, trumpet-tongued, against
The deep damnation of his taking-off.

English, yes—but let's pause for a bit: just how does one
"bear one's faculties" or be "clear" in one's office? "Taking-
off"—where to? And remember, this is about hearing these
lines spoken live. What follows is the passage in Conrad
Spoke's translation, changing only those words that can no
longer speak to us (about 10 percent, according to the linguist David Crystal and his son, the actor Ben Crystal, who

have advised the Globe Theatre in London on the original pronunciation of Shakespeare's plays):

> Besides, this Duncan
> Hath borne authority so meek, hath been
> So pure in his great office, that his virtues
> Will plead like angels, trumpet-tongued, against
> The deep damnation of his knocking-off.

This is hardly a desecration. The language is still challenging and even beautiful, especially since most of it is the original. The difference is simply that words that today only a scholar can hear live and understand have been replaced with ones that all educated people can hear with meaning. The translation is not "pure Shakespeare," but there is an argument that the trade-off is worth it: quite simply, *authority* and *knocking-off* allow us to understand what the man is saying.*

Neither I nor anyone else wants to see the original plays withdrawn from circulation. However, a world where the usual experience of a Shakespeare play outside universities was in today's English would be one where, quite simply, more people were capable of truly understanding and enjoying the Bard's work rather than genuflecting to it. Seeing

---

* I can't resist. In response to my Shakespeare argument, Crystal *père et fils* state that only about 10 percent of Shakespeare's words defy modern comprehension. Interesting that the word *decimate*, to reduce by 10 percent, came so readily to mean "to utterly destroy"! That is, my riposte to them is that one word in ten is enough to render comprehension in live performance often elusive.

Shakespeare shouldn't be like eating your vegetables—
even tasty vegetables. Nor is it much more inspiring for us
to treat Shakespeare as a kind of verbal wallpaper or scent
that we sit back and allow to "wash over" us. I highly suspect Shakespeare himself, hearing so many today espousing
this approach to his words, would have been at best
bemused and at worst disappointed. Shakespeare translated into today's English wouldn't be exactly Shakespeare,
no. But given a choice between Shakespeare as an elite
taste and Shakespeare engaged the way Russians engage
Chekhov and Americans engage Scorsese films and *Arrested
Development*, some may judge Shakespeare that isn't always
exactly what Shakespeare wrote as less than a tragedy.

I have been pleased to see that since the 1990s, when I
first laid down my own case for the translation of Shakespeare, the notion seems to have gained a certain amount of
traction. Mr. Spoke, as well as Kent Richmond of California
State University, Long Beach, have actually executed translated versions of the plays, and as I write, the Oregon Shakespeare Festival has commissioned modern translations of
the entire corpus. To the extent that the approach gathers
steam, many will certainly decry it as desecration, a symptom of the dumbing down of American society. However,
others will feel that translating Shakespeare is a pragmatic
response to the fact that language always changes, and that
when it comes to Shakespeare, quite simply, it's been a while.

In the Present: "What's the Ask?" over "What's the Request?"

To understand that words are always moving along also helps us understand things happening in the language today. In America, an interesting novelty especially popular among young corporate types is the use of basic verbs as nouns, as in "What's the ask?" about business transactions, "Is there a solve?" instead of "Is there a solution?," and "Epic fail." The last has spread far beyond the cubicle realm, and "I know that feel" (instead of "I know how that feels" or "I know that feeling") is even associated with "bros" rather than Dilberts.

A linguist's first observation must be that English speakers have been transforming verbs into nouns this way for a good thousand years. English is low on endings that show what part of speech a word is; in French the -er in *parler* shows that it is a verb and in Spanish the -ar in *hablar* shows the same thing, but in English, nothing about the word *talk* shows that it is a verb. This means that it's easy to use English verbs as nouns—they don't seem as out of place in the role as would a French or Spanish verb, with its verbal ending hanging out inconveniently. Those who assail turning verbs into nouns as inappropriate may not realize that they should also, to be consistent, disapprove of sentences like "She had a funny walk," "He has a scratch next to his eye," and "They simply had too much work." *Walk, scratch,* and *work* all started as verbs.

Yet one might still feel that "What's the ask?" is different, in that the word *request* already exists. Why "Epic fail" when we have *failure*, or "What's the solve?" when we have *solution*? However, today's nouns from verbs are not substitutes for older nouns; they are new words entirely. This is because the older words, as words, have always been drifting in their meanings, and therefore no longer mean exactly what their "vanilla" definition suggests.

Solution, for instance, technically means "a solving." However, the word has, in its journey as a normal word, taken on certain implications. *Solution* brings to mind, for one, math, and overall has an air of the schoolroom about it, as in solutions to science class homework. Those unspoken associations are not what the modern adult in the flinty, competitive atmosphere of a business meeting means. Subconsciously that person reaches for a word that really does mean, in clean fashion, a "solving." What handier way is there to do this than using *solve* itself? But this means that a solve and a solution are subtly different things, in terms of how the words feel in an intimate way to native speakers.

In the same way, a failure and a fail are not the same thing. *Failure* is not, in terms of how it is used in actual speech, simply the act of failing. It once was, but over time it has taken on a whiff of personal condemnation. *Failure* suggests, most readily, a rather large-scale, tragic kind of failing; one thinks of an assessment of a person's entire career, marriage, or life, of a head hung low, and the plays of Arthur Miller. "Epic failure!" then, is a little mean. In modern English, the actual word for simply "a failing," with no ominous hint of therapy sessions or a gun going off offstage, is "a fail." It's certainly handier for people playing video games or rating one another's sales volume.

It's no surprise that men are best known for "I know that feel." *Feeling* has associations with vulnerability, for one. Plus, the word *feeling* is probably most spontaneously associated with the idiom "That hurt my feelings," which is these days, for better or worse, often associated with a certain triviality or tinniness. *Feel* lends a way to use the same *feel* root without the distracting associations. Call it "bro'ly love," also extendable to other younger people wary of excess sentiment (i.e., seeking the "cool"—and note that *cool* and *coolness*, too, have different meanings).

In the Future: Making Peace with the Euphemism Treadmill

When we understand that words inevitably drift in their meanings, then we know why terminology fashioned for euphemistic reasons tends to require constant replacement. What begins as a willfully objective designation is quickly associated in the mind with the phenomenon it refers to, complete with the less savory resonances thereof. As a result, that term comes to have a different meaning than what was intended. In response, a new, faceless term is created—which naturally itself becomes accreted with the same associations and must in time yield to a new term.

It's easy to see some kind of shell game going on, but really, it's just words behaving the way they always have and always will. In a distant day long ago, when a family survived on money from the government, it was popularly called *home relief*, a neutral and benevolent term. However, anyone old enough to have known that term will have to work to imagine *home relief* in its "dictionary" meaning, because quickly *home relief* took on connotations associated with uncomplimentary assumptions about the poor. *Welfare* was thought to be a less pejorative term and became the preferred usage in the 1960s. Again, however, these days it can be sobering to imagine that the word *welfare* refers technically to, simply, being okay. *Welfare* became rusted with so many associations amid the culture wars of the 1980s and '90s that, since then, *cash assistance* has been making new strides into the language as yet another attempt to refer to, well, home relief without setting off alarms.

Note that if you are too young to have known the time when *home relief* was a common term, today it sounds quite handy as a replacement for *welfare*. Perhaps it should be recycled as the next term of art when *cash assistance* takes on abusive tones and becomes dispreferred. We can be quite sure it will—for the same reason that Shakespeare meant "knowledge" by *wit*, and *epic failure* would not mean the same thing as *epic fail*. All these things are of a piece.

In the same way, we must expect that designations for various groups will turn over regularly: the linguist and psychologist Steven Pinker has perfectly titled this "the euphemism treadmill." Long ago, *crippled* was thought a humane way to describe a person—it had the ring, roughly, that *hindered* would today. However, once it became associated with the kind of ridicule tragically common among members of our species, *handicapped* was thought to be a kinder term—less loaded, it sounded like a title rather than a slur. But while words change, people often don't—naturally, after a while, *handicapped* seemed as smudged by realities as *crippled* had. Hence: *disabled*, which is now getting old, as in having taken on many of the same negative associations as *crippled* and *handicapped*. Of late, some prefer *differently abled*, which is fine in itself. Yet all should know that in roughly a generation's time, even that term will carry the very associations it is designed to rise above, just as *special needs* now does. Note the effort now required to imagine how objective and inclusive even *special needs* was fashioned to be.

And here's the rub: since words cannot help drifting in their meanings, we need not worry that people are deliberately keeping us off guard or are given to indecision. The euphemism treadmill must be accepted as an inevitable and unexceptionable result of what a word is: not only a bundle of sounds linked to a meaning, but also one that naturally piles up with implications over time because it is used by human beings living lives. Since words can't sit still, and the implications they attract will sometimes be unpleasant, civility will require changing some of them regularly, like underwear.

But That Isn't What It's Supposed to Mean!

A word is a thing on the move. This means wrapping our heads around something that cannot feel right at first, but that simple logic requires us to accept. To wit, any claim that people in general are using a word "erroneously" is illogical. Of course if the issue is just one person using a word in an unprecedented way, then we might classify it as a mistake. A language is a contract under which there is general, although unconscious, agreement as to where words are moving. To use a word in a fashion that impedes communication with others is therefore a foul. However, mistakes of that kind will usually come from children or foreigners. If a significant proportion of the people speaking a language are using a word in a way that dictionaries tend not to mention, it means that the word is moving—as we would expect, since words always do.

A quick example: *Decimate,* it is true, first meant killing one in ten of an army's men as a postvictory punishment. The source was the Latin word for ten, such that the truly original meaning may actually have been "tithe," as in a tax of 10 percent of one's earnings. Either way, *decimate* originally had a very particular meaning, the knowledge of which pleases a person who knows Latin.

This, however, is strictly a historical matter. There are those given to treating it as "wrong" for someone to say, "A virus decimated the ladybug population and after a few years there were none to be found." They complain that the word should not be used to mean general destruction, but only the subtraction of precisely a tenth. That today *destruction* is pretty much the only usage of *decimate* is, according to this complaint, beside the point. Majority does not entail truth, after all: there is a general waywardness afoot, with the flock losing touch with that real meaning of "to subtract by a tenth." H. W. Fowler's doughty old *A Dictionary*

of Modern English Usage, cherished over generations as authoritative, intoned that sentences like *A single frosty night decimated the currants by as much as 80 percent* "must be avoided."

Okay—but only if you want to avoid using *merry* to
mean "jolly" and will be okay with talking about someone
who, after slimming down on a diet, after a while *reduced*
back up to his former weight. What's the difference between
then and now, except that the older things happened when
nobody was complaining? *Decimate* moved—it broadened
from meaning "to shave off by a tenth" to referring to more
general destruction. Part of the reason, one suspects, is that
since ancient times, with their rather barbaric attitudes
toward human life, existence offers relatively little need for
the concept of reducing something by specifically a tenth:
"Oh, sweetie, make sure to *decimate* the cake so that Maude
can have her slice before the other nine of us!"

So, one answer to the observation "But wasn't it nice to
have a way to express that concept?" is: not really, and
anyone who wants one anyway has it at the ready. One
can say "reduce by a tenth." Hopefully one will do so in
comfort with the knowledge that *reduce* once had a different
meaning—while *comfort* was once "to make strong," and
strong once meant "narrow"!

It's always a safe bet that a word will not be tomorrow
what it is today. In fact, sometimes words don't just change
their meaning—they lose their independence and become
parts of brand-new words entirely.

3

When Words Stop Being Words

Where Does Grammar Come From?

There was a time when to name a girl Amber was like naming her Isabella or Chloe today. It had a hint of novelty and panache, rather than the tinnier air it has taken on since. Starting in the late 1940s, the name Amber was a novelty because of a best-selling novel, which a prim lady on a park bench is reading in a Sylvester and Tweety cartoon of the era. The woman is repeatedly shocked by what she is reading (titled just *Amber* in the cartoon, but audiences would have gotten the reference), in line with *Forever Amber*'s notoriety as a "dirty" book. The novel made the name Amber fashionable. There's a reason there was no such thing as a flapper, Gilded Age matron, or early First Lady named Amber.

Yet today there isn't a thing in *Forever Amber*, a kind of poor man's *Vanity Fair*, that would even raise eyebrows.

A paragraph ends with "then his head bent and he blew out the last candle," after which the next paragraph begins, "From the beginning Amber had both half-hoped and half-feared that she would become pregnant"; or elsewhere similarly, "As they lay in the bed, her head resting on his shoulder . . ." Never does the author, Kathleen Winsor, venture to actually describe what had gone on between her characters. Yet this book was considered hot peppers in its day, enough to make that cartoon matron gasp.

But to keep making money shocking the public with sex, pop culture had to push the envelope ever more. In 1981 a woman I think I was on a date with dragged us out of a showing of *Body Heat* because of its early scene of Kathleen Turner and William Hurt's characters having sex, something that would have sounded like science fiction when *Forever Amber* was published. Yet today, scenes like that are ordinary not only in the movies but on much of television; to make an impression, things must get even more creative.

The Signal Fades

It does. Or the joke that was convulsingly funny loses its snap and must be replaced by a new one. The fashion that turned heads then is now old news. There was a time when it was a tangy gesture to sport what were as often called "dungarees," but today it's wearing something *other* than jeans in casual settings that is the statement, if anything.

And of course, things are much the same in language. It is often remarked that people are now using multiple exclamation points in texting, social media, and casual writing contexts more than they used to. A Carl's Jr. restaurant receipt, for example, requests, "PLEASE LET US KNOW HOW WE DID!!!" and there are those who consider three exclamation points a standard number for proper texting (OMG!!!). Yet the question "Why are people using so many exclamation points?," implying an unusual quotient of enthusiasm apparently afoot, misses the fact that today three exclamation points means what just one exclamation point did originally.

The reason for the proliferation? The potency of the single exclamation point has faded over time. Originally intended to indicate surprise or emphasis, the exclamation point has seen its connotation diluted in the same way, and for the same reason, that a joke fades, a fashion ceases to distract, or shock value diminishes. A marker once used to summon attention can now be used merely to show that you're *paying* attention, in places where an old-fashioned Strunk and White sensibility would use just a period.

Proper texting, then, requires "See you there!" even from someone who has no reason to be excited about your presence. "See you there" without the exclamation point would imply a shrug or a sneer, and texters are quick to tell you that using a period—"See you there."—conveys virtual hostility. "See you there!" signals not excitement but basic chirpy courtesy.

This is not as novel as it seems, either: it has long been a convention in many comic books to mark characters' statements with exclamation points rather than periods. Old issues of *Archie* were typical in this: one story opens with

Veronica coming upon Archie on his way to go fishing. The dialogue:

ARCHIE: You can watch me if you like!

VERONICA: Oh, I don't want to watch! I'd like to fish, too! Go and get a pole for me!

ARCHIE: You fish? You're joking! You don't know the first thing about it!

There isn't a period at the end of a sentence in the whole episode, and that was par for the course in the *Archie* world. Yet normal people do not shout their conversation. "I'D LIKE TO FISH, TOO!" in real life would get us near water with no one but ourselves. As far back as these comic books, exclamation points were used to indicate, essentially, basic engagement.

Nor is this solely about America. Scandinavians have long used exclamation points after people's names when beginning a letter or, today, e-mail, note, etc. To them, this usage connotes what an English speaker indicates with "Dear," and nothing more exclamatory than that. It used to throw me a bit in my interactions with Scandinavians. The e-mail headed "John!" always sounded pleasantly enthusiastic but left me wondering whether I would be able to justify the excitement in person. Today, knowing to read the exclamation point as a wave of the hand, I know that the Swede or Norwegian won't mind if I am just (sniff!) myself.

We have already seen that there is a theme of weakening signals in how words move through time. The firmly objective meaning becomes more elusively subjective: the command of *You must be up by seven o'clock* becomes the internal surmise of *That must be the woman I saw the other day.* The directness of the semantic becomes the abstraction of the pragmatic, as in the difference between doing something well and *Well, horses run fast.* The general goes narrow: *audition* means "hearing" and comes to mean trying out for a performance part, within which hearing will be but a minor thread.

When a Word Devolves into a Tool

Along those lines, we are now prepared to see another possible fate of a word. A language is more than just a basket of words—you could know five thousand of them in a language and be miserably unable to communicate even the most basic of sentiments without also knowing how to put the words together. A language is not only its words but also its grammar.

We are most familiar with the concept of grammar in terms of endings, such as the *-ed* that marks the past, the *-s* that marks the plural noun and the third person singular verbs, and the *-ing* that makes a verb progressive. However, grammar also includes what are still, technically, words. For example, *the* and *a,* our definite and indefinite articles: *the* pear refers to a pear already discussed, while *a* pear refers to a pear freshly brought into the conversation. Yet while *the* and *a* are, because they stand alone, words, note that this difference between the definite and the indefinite is a matter of grammar, in the same way as marking the plural or the past tense is. The word *the* doesn't "mean" something in the same way that the word *pear* does. The foreigner asks "What does *the* mean?" and your answer, to the extent that you can manage one, will be quite different from explaining what *giraffe* or *temporary* "means." Your answer would likely start with "Well, you use *the* to . . ."—that is, you *use* it, whereas you wouldn't say you "use" *giraffe* to refer to a bizarrely long-necked and silent animal. To master how to use *the* is part of learning how to put words together—that is, grammar. Like *-ed* and *-s*, *the* and *a* are tools. Grammar is partly prefixes and suffixes, but it is also some things that stand by themselves as separate words. That is, there are "word" words (*pear, okapi, rhombus*) and then grammar words (*the, a, and, or, may, would*).

The question is, though: where does the grammar come from?

You are an early human sitting under a tree with no language at all, who has never even encountered a language, but hankers with the desire to create one. You will naturally assign names to things like trees, to actions like climbing them, and even to descriptions of the trees, such as "green." But if you want to be able to say that something happened in the past, the last thing you will do is hatch up an ending to snap on to verbs. Remember, you've never known a language, so endings aren't something you've ever encountered. Spontaneously you would seek a *word* to express the past just like you've made up words for everything else. Maybe something like *yesterday*, or *behind*—but certainly not coming up with something as queer as an ending that can't stand by itself and glomming it onto some other word.

We don't need to just surmise about what you would do, either. There have been rare cases when people have had to build a language from the ground up, such as when slaves were brought to plantations and heard a few hundred words of the master's language and forged that into a brand-new language, called a creole. When people in circumstances like this never got much exposure to the colonizer language and really had to make a new language by themselves, they didn't make up endings to indicate things like the past or the plural. Instead, they lassoed in a *word* to mean the past or the plural (for the latter, often *them* or *all*). So where do endings come from?

The answer is the subject of this chapter: another possible fate of a word is that it can gradually, without anyone noticing it over time, go from being a word to being a piece of grammar. Endings, as a rule, start as words; becoming an ending happens only later, amid a kind of extended obsolescence. Even grammar in the form of words, such as *the*, *a*, etc., starts as regular words: *the* started as *that*, *a* started as *one*. One result of words never staying the same, then, is that some of them provide the material for what becomes the language's grammar, the blood coursing through its organs.

As always, when we can see this process happening in our actual lives, it's as disturbing as thinking too hard about your sibling's or child's dating experiences. Yet as with that and so much else involved in life, as queasy as it might make us, we wouldn't want it *not* to happen.

The Way It Used to Be: "Using to" What?

It can be unsettling to be told to think about the fact that you have a tongue in your mouth. It's wet; it's biggish when you consider the whole thing all the way back; plus, it has that pebbly texture you'd find hideous to encounter in some undersea creature. Yet there it is sitting in your mouth and you can't get it out.

There are things we say all day long every day that are deeply weird like that, and one that often occurs to me is the vastly peculiar *used to*, so seldom singled out and yet certainly one of the oddest things in the English language if taken literally. If a sentence is merely a matter of words, then how about *She used to live in Columbus*? We all know *use* as a word, but in what sense is it contributing its meaning in *She used to live in Columbus*? She wasn't using anything, or at least that isn't what the sentence means.

Even the way we say *used to* gives away that more is going on than our simply saying the word *use*. Imagine someone pronouncing the *used to* in that sentence as "yuzed to," the way we would pronounce *used* in *She used a pen*. But no—to say "She yuuuzed to live in Columbus" would sound distinctly oleaginous; no one would even venture it. The thoroughly correct pronunciation of *used to* in the sense intended in *She used to live in Columbus* is "yoosta." One might venture "yoostu" to preserve the pronunciation of the *to*, but the *used* part has to be "yoos," not "yooz."

Used to is, then, something quite different from *use*. Spelling gives away that *used to* ("yoosta") was once—*used to* be!—a form of *use*. But it isn't now, and the difference is that *use* is a "word" word while *used to* ("yoosta") is grammar. *Use* is a word meaning to utilize. *Used to* is, on the other hand, a tool we use to express that something happened on a habitual basis in the past. It fulfills a function right alongside the *-ed* suffix we use to express the simple past: simple past is *he talked*; the past in a continuous way is *he used to talk*. To anyone who has taken French or Spanish, this difference will recall the two choices of past in those languages, such as the preterite and imperfect in Spanish: he talked once: *habló*; he was talking: *hablaba*. In an alternate universe, English would also have an ending to indicate the "imperfect" to parallel the *-ed* one, but that just happens not to be the way things worked out.

The path from *use* to "yoosta" begins with the kinds of changes we saw in the previous chapter, of the kind that take "blessed" through "innocent" and "weak" to "silly." When it comes to using something, chances are you don't use it just once. Typically one makes use of something regularly, over a long period of time—use is something one most readily thinks of as long-term: usage, as it were. That reality hovered over *use*, to the point that long-term usage (habit) became a secondary meaning of the word. A nice example is Thomas Hobbes in *The Leviathan* intoning in 1651, "Long use obtaineth the authority of a law," where *use* could be substituted for by *practice* or *habit*. Set phrases of the period such as *use and custom* and *as the use is* (which meant "which is the usual") further indicated this new meaning.

Aware of this meaning, we can more easily understand Late Middle English sentences such as a record from 1550 that one *Thomas Casberd has used to set his cart in the street.*

(In the actual spelling: "Thomas Casberd hathe vsid to sett his carte in the streate.") That meant, Mr. Casberd "used," as in, *had the custom of*, parking in the street. Or John Milton, in 1670, wrote in his history of England about "the English then useing to let grow on their upper-lip large mustachio's."

So, to an English speaker of this time, *use* could mean "have the habit of," or to translate into modern slang, "has this thing where he . . ." From here, the path to today's "yoosta" is clearer than if we just start with the "utilize" meaning. Over time, the meaning generalized, such that one could say *used to* to refer not only to someone harboring a habit, but also to habitual or ongoing things themselves, regardless of who, if anybody, was responsible for them. In 1550, *Thomas Casberd has used to set his cart in the street* referred to Casberd's having regularly executed an action, and Milton's mustachioed men did that to their faces on purpose. However, *She used to live in Columbus* doesn't refer to the woman regularly executing the action of living in Columbus, which wouldn't even make sense. It refers to her having lived in Columbus ongoingly. One can now also say something like *Based on this data, she used to be the only person with type O blood in the village*, when the woman in question didn't even know what her blood type was and/or certainly wasn't performing the action of having that blood type once a day. Her blood type just was what it was, and as something that didn't change, was an ongoing state—hence *used to*. *Used to* doesn't even have to be about a living being: *My cello used to have a richer sound*. Cellos don't have customs.

Used to has gone from meaning "was in the habit of doing" to, well, "yoosta." We use "yoosta" whether the issue is a deliberate action (*He used to ski*), a passive state of being (*He used to hallucinate*), or anything that was ongoing in the past (*It used to be easier to find a mailbox*, where the "it" in question is too abstract to imagine practicing anything or having habits). *I liked it the way it used to be*—again, how could this abstract "it" do anything habitually in the way that Thomas Casberd did? *Used to* is now not a word but a tool, one that puts a statement into the past habitual: a piece of grammar.*

Grammar and *Modern Family* (Just Read On!)

The proper analogy is with a certain trend in television sitcoms. *The Office* was based on a conceit that a documentary was being made, such that the plots were regularly interrupted by sequences where the characters talked to the camera alone or in pairs in the style of reality shows. In the American version of the show, at a point of high drama certain characters even turned their mikes off for privacy, and in one plot arc in the final season the cameramen were actually shown, with one of them harboring a crush on Pam.

In the wake of *The Office*, the sitcoms *Modern Family* and

---

* This new meaning, *practice*, yielded another development of *use*: to practice was to become accustomed, or to accustom someone else. The mother seal will be seen, a book of natural history noted in 1783, to "use her little ones to live under water," meaning to accustom them to it, not to exploit them. When in 1826 a woman is said to have taken a man and "used him in her company," it can seem rather bawdy unless we know that the writer meant "accustomed him to her company." Here, then, is the source of the expression *to be used to* something, quite an oddity if we think of *use* with the meaning of "utilize."

Parks and Recreation also had characters regularly doing mini-monologues to the camera. However, on these shows there was no pretense that a documentary was being made. Instead, there was a tacit expectation that television audiences were now accustomed to the sitcom narrative sprinkled with off-line commentary by the characters, such that the soliloquy commentaries could now simply help flesh out the storytelling as a kind of abstract extra layer. The soliloquies were recast on these later shows as what film scholarship would call part of the *grammar* of the show, alongside long-established techniques such as the close-up, the cross-cut, and the splicing in of sentimental soundtrack music.

The relationship between *use* and "yoosta" is equivalent. If you don't happen to be into sitcoms, jeans are again apropos. Once upon a time, ripping your jeans was quite the rebellion—"Ha! I can wear my clothes all torn up and whaddaya gonna do about it!" Today, the ripping is, especially among women, just one of many things that are considered to make jeans look acceptable. The rips, like the height of the waist and the flare at the bottom, are part of how jeans go from being a pair of pants to making a statement, as it were: the denim grammar.

The point is that today's grammar words are born from regular words changing: what we associate with the "rules" of English began as the kinds of ordinary words those rules apply to. For example, here is the quintessence of "grammar": a passage from the grandfather of all old-time grammatical descriptions of English, Robert Lowth's once-classic *A Short Introduction to English Grammar*, written in 1762. Here Lowth describes, in the grand old fashion derived from Latin textbooks (*as was the use* at the time) certain aspects of grammar. In this era, it was also still *the use* to write most *s*'s as what look like *f*'s, so for authenticity's sake I will preserve those,* as well as the printer's use of capitals and italics:

The *Poffibility* of a thing depends upon the power of its caufe; and may be expreffed,

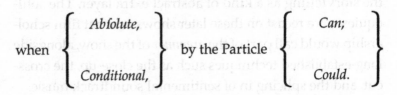

when $\left\{ \begin{array}{l} \textit{Abfolute,} \\ \textit{Conditional,} \end{array} \right\}$ by the Particle $\left\{ \begin{array}{l} \textit{Can;} \\ \textit{Could.} \end{array} \right\}$

The Neceffity of a thing from fome *external Obligation*, whether *Natural* or *Moral*, which we call Duty, is expreffed,

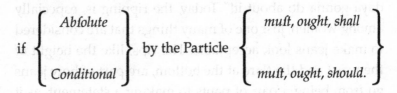

if $\left\{ \begin{array}{l} \textit{Abfolute} \\ \textit{Conditional} \end{array} \right\}$ by the Particle $\left\{ \begin{array}{l} \textit{muft, ought, shall} \\ \textit{muft, ought, should.} \end{array} \right\}$

Very nice, but from a presentation like this, especially with the solemn, incantatory language, it seems as if these

---

* And yes, because it looks funny now. But it wasn't actually an *f*, but a long stroke that was often decorated with a little left-hanging scarf. Observe, blown up a bit: ſ. This does makes it look so much like an *f*, however, that frankly our confusion and amusement today must be judged the ancients' fault.

"particles" emerged from on high in their current state. However, descriptions like this, in their lists of "particles," actually capture ordinary words at one point amid their changes over time.

Take *ought*. One may think of tongues again in having occasion to zero in on this strange little seal-yelp of a word, with its clotty spelling making it look like something somebody punched. *Ought* once was, of all things, the past tense of *owe*. In Shakespeare's *Henry IV, Part 1*, you can see it used in both the present and the past. Mistress Quickly tells Prince Hal that Falstaff "said this other day you *ought* him a thousand pound." The prince asks Falstaff, "Sirrah! Do I *owe* you a thousand pound?"

But when you owe, you're under an obligation. The obligation is most readily thought to be financial or transactional, but one way the word might change is for the sense of obligation to become more general. There was a time when *ought* was often interpretable as meaning either "owed," the basic sense, or "obligated," in a more general one, as in a twelfth-century passage about God (with the Early Middle English rendered as Modern): "For he made all creatures, and nevertheless the world didn't know him as it *ahhte*," with *ahhte* at this time translatable either as "owed" or "ought." The world didn't know God in the way that it owed it to him to do, which is close to saying "as it ought." After a while, *ought* came to refer unambiguously to what you should do in a general sense, which alongside words like *may*, *must*, and *should*, is a grammar word. Meanwhile, a new regular past tense form using the *-ed* ending, *owed*, took the place once occupied by *ought*, which had now moved on to, as it were, grammar pastures.

"Can you hear what I hear?"—now sing to the same tune "*Can's* a piece of graaammar . . ." As grammar, it presumably started as something else, and it did: *cunnan* in Old English meant "know." Ben Jonson in *The Magnetic Lady* has Mistress Polish praise a deceased woman for the fact that "She could the Bible in the holy tongue." We can't help at first suspecting a typo—she could what? But *could* meant, all by itself, "knew." There was even an old expression "to can by heart" alongside our familiar "know by heart." Modern English is littered with remnants of that stage: other offshoots of *cunnan* are *cunning* and *canny*, all about having your wits about you. Plus, the past tense of *cunnan* was a word pronounced "coothe," from which the *couth* in *uncouth* comes: the uncouth person is lacking in know-how, as in the kind that lends one social graces.

But if you know, it follows that you are able, and along those lines, *can* voyaged from the concreteness of knowing to the abstractness of indicating general ability: Yes, We Can!

Or one more: *Let's go!* What are the words in that sentence? Technically, *let*, *us*, and *go*. But are we really using the word *let*? If we are asking to be let to go, then who was holding us back? *Let go of me! Let it alone! Let it run down!* We can't say we are using *let* in those senses when we say, *Let's go*, nor are we really saying *us* when we say the *'s* part. Spelling, as always, deceives: the spelling of *let's* makes it look like a contraction of *let* and *us*, which it once was—but things have changed. While it feels perfectly natural to say *is not* instead of *isn't*, notice that saying *Let us go* feels like we're doing bad Shakespeare. In barely any real-life situation, no matter how careful a speaker one is, would one say, "Let us go."

That's because *let's* is no longer *let+us*. *Let's* is a piece of grammar. It refers not to the action of letting, but to the function of encouragement. Lowth puts it, "*Let* does not only exprefs* permiffion; but praying, exhorting, commanding." Exactly: all languages have a way of rallying the troops in that way. It's a command applied to us rather than someone else, a musty but useful term for it being the hortative. Languages like Latin and the Romance languages do it by putting a verb in the subjunctive: ¡*Viva Zapata!*, "May Zapata live!" in which the *-a* ending on *vivir* signifies the subjunctive mood. Other languages have a little separate word to do it, or a suffix, or any number of strategies. English's is a little grammar word that by all rights should be spelled "letz."

When Words Lose Their Selves: Grammaticalization Goes Further

Notice that I am sneaking that term in. *Grammaticalization* is what linguists call it when a word becomes a piece of grammar. I have avoided using the word until now because it's tempting to think it has something to do with grammaticality in the sense of proper phrasing. It also sounds, with its seven clattering syllables, generally intimidating, or at

---

* The rule was that you didn't use the funny *s* at the end of a word.

least like some kind of problem. Some use *grammaticization*, but that isn't much better. Yet, here we are, and there's certainly no better term I can think of myself.

The grammaticalization process can go further than *ought* and *let's*. When a word no longer has meaning per se, and is more something used to organize the words that do have meaning, it no longer gets accented much. *You used to be the only one*: the melody is "YOU used to be the OWN-ly ONE." The *used to*, and the other grammar word *the*, are mumbled compared to the *you* and the *only* and the *one*, the "word" words. (*Be* is a whole story in itself, not as much a "real" word as we have reason to suppose.) You could possibly say, "You USED TO be the OWN-ly ONE," but that's only for emphasis, the unusual case.

Now add the fact that grammar words tend to be used an awful lot. You can't talk without using the grammar to put words together, and so *used to, the,* and *a* get much heavier wear-and-tear than *umbrella, squirt,* or *avoid*. So: we have a word usually mumbled rather than accented, and used that way day in and day out by countless people over vast periods of time. Two things can happen to a word like that.

First, it starts sounding different, losing the ringing, robust sound of solid words like *goat, jolly,* and *deodorant*. Second, in that weakened state it starts leaning, as it were, against a robust "real" word next to it. After a while, it gets accustomed to that and can no longer stand up on its own at all. Or, to step back from the anthropomorphizing, when something is said without an accent and uttered constantly, we can start to hear it as a syllable of a word next to it, rather than being its own word. Think of a toolshed. We don't think of it as a building, precisely, even though it technically is. Small, uninsulated, of narrow purpose, and ugly, it's an appendage to a house, an architectural punctuation, even if it isn't actually adjacent to the house. You'd never build a toolshed by itself out in the middle of a field, and in fact, one might be nagged by a sense that if a toolshed isn't right up against the house, it kind of should be. It's not really a building, after all. In fact, a garage might seem a better bet—keeps everything nice and connected.

A heavily used little grammar word has a way of becoming a toolshed. After a while, it actually is a syllable of other words, and can never stand alone—the birth of a prefix or suffix. A good example is the *-ly* that forms adverbs like *slowly* and *gently*. It started as the word *like* (pronounced "leek" back then). That's easy to imagine because even today we can still say *slow-like* to mean "in a slow fashion." Used that way constantly, however, *like* lost the accent it once had. You hit the *like* in *slow-like* fairly hard, but the *-ly* in *slowly* not so much. Mumbled, it lost its final consonant— "leek" became "lee." And in that state, where it no longer even sounded like what it had originally been, it became easy to hear this "lee" as something hanging off *slow* rather than its own word, as something hanging off *warm, quick, light*, etc.—until now there became an adverbial suffix *-ly* that no one would ever associate with *like* except scholars of language change who know where the bodies are buried. (As it happens, *like* originated as a word meaning *body*!)

What becomes a word, then, can wind up as a mere syllable. The suffix *-hood* in *childhood, motherhood,* and *neighborhood* sounds familiar in its way, because there is a word *hood*. We might think that these words are simply double-decker words like *blackboard* and *cheeseburger*. However, the word *hood* as we know it doesn't mean "condition" as it does in these longer words. If what we know as *hood* were the source, then *neighborhood* would refer to the person next door's shawl, an unlikely thing to have a word for at all. And as for the now well-known slang term '*hood* for *neighborhood*, clearly that term arose long after *childhood*, *motherhood*, and the others. No one was calling themselves "from the 'hood" during the Iron Age.

The *-hood* suffix is actually from an Old English word pronounced "hod." It meant "condition" or, by extension, "manner" or "way." In *Beowulf*, Grendel gets hurt through *hæstne had*—"violent means," as in "in a violent way." However, used next to words like *child*, *mother*, and *neighbor*, *hod* morphed into *-hood*. Today's term *the 'hood* technically means, then, "the condition"—go figure.

This kind of story is in the past of most suffixes and prefixes. The *-ed* that marks the past probably started as *did*: *painted* goes back, in other words, to *paint-did*. Considering how often you refer to things in the past, you could have known that *did*, when used that way, was eventually going to wear down to something like an *-ed*, inseparable from the verb itself.*

---

* I'm cheating a little again. Old English itself already had this past tense suffix in place. Really, the word for *did* would have glommed onto the verbs in English's ancestor, also the ancestor to the other languages of English's subfamily, Germanic, all of which have a similar past tense suffix. Linguists call that language Proto-Germanic; we will likely never know

Didn't You Use to Be Somebody?
When the Journey Ends

The life cycle I am depicting can include, as you may have suspected, that stage we don't like to talk about: demise. When what is now just an appendix to other words, unaccented and barely thought of as language, is uttered incessantly enough over a long enough period of time, it can just plain wear out and fade away.

This is what happened with English verbs, to such an extent that the only signs left of what once was are peeking out from behind the curtains of the language, as unnoticeable as the dust specks in the air that you catch sight of only when the light is slanting in just the right way.

Here are some Old English verbs. You don't have to know or care a thing about Old English to notice that all the verbs have one thing in common:

shake	ahrysian
rattle	hrutan
roll	wealcan
wash	wæscan
rinse	aþierran
repeat	geedlæcan

---

what its speakers called it because they didn't have writing. But we can know that they likely said "walk-did," "help-did," etc.

It's that they all end in *-an*. All verbs in Old English did: the *-an* (or sometimes *-on*) was what marked something as a verb, just as *-ly* marks something as an adverb today, but much more consistently. (The ending *-ly* is used often, but not always, as we know from adverbs like *often* and *always!*) Readers who have studied German will be familiar with the way verbs in that language end in *-en*; Old English, sister language to German, had the same feature.

But the *-an* was unaccented: the word for rattle, *hrutan*, was pronounced HROO-tahn. Or, after a while, more like HROO-tun, with the vowel sound in the *-an* ending drifting from *ah* into the grubbier kind of sound such as the *o* in *lemon*. As time went by, the *-n* dropped off and left just that little vowel alone. It was even more vulnerable to the elements than when it was protected by an *-n*, and during the Middle English period it wore away completely. From then on, English had no ending to show that something was a verb.

Today, the old *-an* ending hangs around on the margins, but it's something that has to be pointed out, like showing someone that deer standing just over the hill fixing to bolt away. Because we have the words *length* and *strength*, we can glean that the *-en* in *lengthen* and *strengthen* serves to make words into verbs. There is also a reason that in older poetry you can catch *ope* for *open*. *Ope* was the natural result of the ending wearing away, but by chance, the old *open* stuck around, kind of like that guy in college who kept visiting after he graduated, maybe a little too often, and after a while got a job on campus and, last you heard, is still there. *Open* was like him: you just couldn't get rid of it, and it ended up becoming the standard form. However, we don't think of the -en in open as a suffix, any more than we think of the -en in listen as one. Listen is another example of the old form happening to hang on—by all rights it "should" be just list, and you can actually find that word in, again, old poems.

But the ending remains a dead thing. We can't make new words with it. Today, even if you are one of the people who reviles the use of nouns like structure as verbs, you certainly aren't wishing people would say "structuren" instead, and I don't recall anyone giving "faxen" a try instead of just saying they needed to fax something. When the founder of The Simpsons' Springfield coined the town motto "A noble spirit embiggens the smallest man," the use of -en where it isn't already established can only register as funny.

Grammaticalization Is Something Happening, Not Something That Happened

A natural question at this point might be: if endings are always wearing away like this, then how does a language keep any grammar around at all? There are two answers.

First, the endings (and prefixes) are not always wearing away. The prefixes and suffixes that are less necessary to making sense are more vulnerable than others, but when there is a bit of stuff that we really need in order to express thoughts, it tends to hold on tight. The Old English verbal ending -an was low on the scale of necessity; it's usually pretty clear that something is a verb from the fact that it refers to an action. However, English is in no hurry to let the past-marking ending -ed wear off, because one achingly needs to refer to the past and, in fact, does so more than one refers to the present or future.

I feel bad for the teacher my elementary school hired to give us Spanish lessons in fourth grade. She deserved major props for actually teaching us the present tense conjugation instead of just a scattering of nouns and expressions, but I kept asking her when we were going to learn to put things in the past, because it seemed to me that every second thing I wanted to say was in the past. But the past in Spanish is harder to teach—I must have gotten on her nerves. Yet within my obnoxiousness I was onto something: you need that past tense to get beyond the "My uncle is a lawyer but my aunt has a spoon" level of things. For example, while it is inherent to casual speech to let some things slide, people make unconscious calculations as to what is expendable. People actually are much more likely to say, "We saw *Wes' Side Story*," letting go of a *t* that has no meaning, than to say, "Yesterday I kiss' my daughter" and leave off the -ed that is so central to basic meaning.

Therefore it isn't that every grammatical bit that isn't accented is ripe for elimination. If you are Jewish and went to Hebrew school, remember being taught (or not!) that you change the verbs' tense by changing their vowels, so that *kotev* is "writes" but *katav* is "wrote"? That's grammar, and it's been hanging on for thousands of years. It's a trait of the languages in Hebrew's family, Semitic, and none of them has just sloughed this stuff off, accented or not.

Beware, in fact, the myth tripping up not only the general

public but many linguists, that languages regularly let all their prefixes and suffixes fall off. This conception is based essentially on the fact that Modern English has so much less noun case marking and verb conjugation than Old English, and that Latin lost its noun case marking when it became the Romance languages. Indeed, while Latin nouns were marked for case in this way (*stella* means *star*):

nominative	stella
genitive	stellae
dative	stella
accusative	stellam
ablative	stella

you would never know any of this from *étoile*, the descendant word in French for "star." The only way you can change it is to plonk on a plural ending *-s* for *étoiles* (and much of the time, even that *-s* isn't pronounced). In French, case is marked in similar fashion as in English, with prepositions like *of* and *to*, and the accusative is all but ignored.

However, this is by no means what happens to languages in general. Around the world, countless languages with case marking like Latin's basically keep it. The typical language is full of "messes" like this and much more, and has been since time immemorial. Languages like Old English and Latin took it all off because they went through periods where they were learned as much by adults as by children, which makes a language less complex than it would normally be.

Old English was never the same after the Viking invaders picked it up starting in the eighth century. Latin changed when imposed upon subjects of the spreading Roman Empire. But these were abnormal circumstances.

Beware, then, the idea that languages regularly go around dropping away the hard stuff and becoming more like English. If this were the case, then wouldn't all languages actually be like English by now, and since they aren't, what's taking them so long? A suffix may wear off, but just as often being a suffix—or a prefix, or a vowel change of the Hebrew kind, or the difference in English between *run* and *ran*—is home base, the homestead, The Way It Always Is.

Now, eventually, as meanings change and also sounds change (as we will see in chapter 4), even a grammatical bit that serves a needed function starts getting jostled out of existence. A piece of grammar doesn't last for, say, tens of thousands of years. However, by then the subject of the second answer to our question comes into play.

Namely, new things are always grammaticalizing as older ones wear away. Grammaticalization is not something that happened long ago; it's something that is happening now, too—part of what it is to be a living language. The same inevitable processes of creeping reinterpretation that make words go personal or just go some other way (as in chapters 1 and 2) are also always at work turning some words into grammar.

The impulse has its roots in the more general fact that, as much as we are condemned for being sloppy and vague in our language usage, humans are deeply committed to explicitness and clarity. In the back of our minds, we are always sprucing the language up, making sure it does the job, like a director regularly working with the cast of a long-running play to keep it fresh. This is the source of words condemned as redundant, such as the famous *irregardless*. One does not technically need the *ir-* when the *-less* of *regardless* already conveys the negation. However, the fact that the reinforced version with *ir-* has been so readily taken up indicates that people want that negation component to be as clear as possible. In the word *overwhelm*, you might wonder why there is no word *whelm*. In fact, there once was. You might wonder what it meant, and it meant . . . "to overwhelm." *Overwhelm* began as redundant as *irregardless*; people were simply being forceful.

Think of how often people today say things like *sink down* and *rise up*, when the verbs themselves, *sink* and *rise*, contain what *down* and *up* contribute. The impulse to add *down* and *up* is one of clarity: *rise up* is stronger, more vivid, than *rise*. One could just do with *rise* if one were, for some reason, limited to expressing only exactly what was necessary with as little expenditure of energy or verbiage as possible. Yet who set this condition for human language? Note how incompatible such puritanical parsimony seems to almost any other endeavor we value or esteem—what art, what culture, what feeling, what ingenuity, what humanity could spring from such a prescription? *Sink down* isn't messy; it breathes, commits, lives. Hence similar constructions one hears, such as *penetrate into* and *separate out*: redundant, yes. But it is integral to being a person to be, to a degree, redundant, something in other contexts called energetic or spirited, and what we might usefully term underlining.

Based on the same impulse, speakers of a language are always coaxing some words into switching sides to become grammar, because having grammar is part of what makes a language communicative. Naturally, then, as the old -*an* verb ending wore away, English started using *to* to mark the infinitive. It isn't that now we have no way of marking something as a verb; it's just that suffixes aren't the only way to do such things. Now we have *to shake, to rattle,* and *to roll.*

Meanwhile, there are other grammaticalizations happening under our noses: a language seems to "want" to fill in a goodly number of slots of experience with a grammatical way of marking it. No language can fill all the slots, and part of the fun is watching which ones a language is filling at any given time. Yet this is a sport few get to watch, because so often the result is condemned as trivial or ridiculous.

An example is the counterexpectational *ass* discussed in chapter 1: *big-ass pot, long-ass movie.* Recall that it is no small feat to explain just how to use *ass* in that way. The reference is not anatomical, and yet it doesn't work to simply say that it means "very" or "more." As we have seen, when something is that hard to put your finger on, like *Well . . .* and the function of *LOL,* that is often a sign that it is no longer a normal word, but grammar. Counterexpectational *ass* is not the "word" word *ass* that it began as. A Martian hearing American English for a week might never happen to hear someone using *ass* to mean *derrière,* but most likely would hear a few counterexpectational *ass* examples. Likely, our Martian would document *ass* as a suffix! After all, it isn't accented—why not *longass* movie, *rottenass* meat? The twentieth century witnessed many interesting things; one of them was the grammaticalization of *ass*.

In Greek, there are different forms of *who* for singular and plural. *Pios?* "Who?" you can ask, about one person, but if you're asking about something two or three people did, then you ask not *Pios?* but *Pii?* And I don't mean Ancient Greek, as if this were something grand but antique about people we'll never know. I mean people walking around in Athens right now. Two *who*s. We just have our measly one: don't you kind of wish we could have two like the Greeks? Wait, we do: the difference between *Who's coming?* and *Who all is coming?* The *all* is a plural marker in that expression, unaccented—it's a piece of grammar, allowing us to pluralize *Who?* as if we were Athenians. *What all* is similar—*I want to know what all I need to do* means, basically, "I want to know the 'whats' I need to do." We are watching *all* become a grammatical marker, possibly even a suffix, and yet we are taught to dismiss it as slang or even as plain wrong.

Yet, if you think about it, any grammaticalization that happens within our experience will be treated that way, for the simple reason that we are taught that language isn't supposed to change—or that it's supposed to change only in that new things need new words. The problem with that analysis is that if people resisting change had their way, we would not have *used to, ought, can,* or *-ly,* which would seem to be strange things to resent at this point.

Grammaticalization as Spectator Sport

From the point of view of one language, such as our own, it will seem as if grammaticalization serves to lend a language the tools it "needs" to convey all shades of meaning. But in fact grammaticalization is driven to a large extent by the same factors of chance that determine how the meanings of words change.

Some words are more subject to grammaticalization than others: *go* and *want*, basic concepts constantly used, are easy to reinterpret as markers of future action, whereas more specific and lesser-used words such as *prickle* and *bloat* never get sought for grammaticalization. However, the concepts that grammaticalization leads to in any given language are not predictable. The phenomenon lends itself to spectating, and perhaps even to betting on the odds of one thing happening over another. So much of our own language's grammar feels so fundamental that it can be surprising how much of it is just arbitrary tinsel that a language could easily do without. An English speaker's sense of what a language is supposed to be is as arbitrary as a mole's sense of what life is supposed to be—there is so very much more out there.

Surely, for example, a language has to have a way of indicating the past tense, so grammaticalization will fulfill that "need," right? Actually, not: plenty of languages have no marker that means the past and get along just fine leaving it to context. It's weird to encounter documentation of such languages—you keep looking in the index, sure that you've missed something, you scan the table of contents again, keep checking random sentences in the book thinking the author must have missed something, but no: there's just no past marker. Some have no markers of past or future. *Most* languages do not have two little grammar words corresponding to our *the* and *a*.

Then, on the other hand, there are languages with grammar that marks things we would never consider as part of a language. Most East Asian and Southeast Asian languages mark the shape of the things you're talking about. Languages on the island of New Guinea tend to have markers that tell whether you're still talking about someone or are switching to discussing someone else. In Native American Algonquian languages, a suffix marks that something had a larger effect on another thing in the sentence than ordinary experience would suggest: if a mouse scared an elephant instead of an elephant scaring a mouse, you'd have to hang that suffix on *scare*. Marking the past or having a word *a* are just a couple of points on a huge roulette wheel.

Hence: just as we saw in chapter 2 that words ooze across a grid of meanings in an endlessly variant array of combinations, grammaticalization creates an endlessly variant array of grammar words marking assorted shades of existence, just "because." Nor, it must be noted, does any of this correlate with the culture of the language's speakers. An attempt to correlate a language's grammatical features with its speakers' cultural traits begins with hope and ends in a sputter.

German, for example, divides its nouns into three genders, usually arbitrarily. Bridges and mortgages are feminine; muffins and purses are masculine; ribbons and udders are neuter. One might ask why German grammaticalized this three-way split in *the*s, such that you have to master the masculine *der*, the feminine *die*, and the neuter *das*. At some point several millennia ago, these gender classes presumably corresponded to some cosmological system among herders or farmers somewhere. No self-regarding humans come up with a system like this just for kicks: even ossified bureaucracies emerge via a series of accidents, not deliberate sabotage, and languages are no different. Presumably, German began as a language like the Australian Dyirbal, in which there were four classes: one for men and most living things; a second for women, water, and fire; a third for fruit and vegetables; and a fourth for everything else.

But the point is that today, German's groups correspond to nothing like this. Whether a noun takes *der*, *die*, or *das* simply has to be learned, dragged along with the logical part of the language like those wedding-day tin cans—and it's a lot of cans: *der*, *die*, and *das* each has different forms for the possessive, the dative, and the object case, and then there are the plural forms, too. Obviously no language "needs" that. Things just drifted into this situation as the old cosmology fell away but the language kept on ticking, carried along because toddlers are capable of picking it up and by the time they are old enough to realize how unnecessary such things are, they are too set in the habit to give it up.

Grammaticalization, then, is accident, and the lesson is crucial. So very much of language is random confluence, despite dictionaries and grammar books giving the illusion of a language as an almost deliberate creation, whose contours are somehow a set, dictated canon. The idea that language is more like cloud formations than the Periodic Table of Elements can be almost unsettling, to be sure. When something is as magnificent as what a whole language is, in all its prolificacy, we *want* it to be "for" something. We hearken to the idea that speakers "built" it via ingenuity and persistence. We reify it, or almost anthropomorphize it, and we're hardly alone, with Russians calling their language "great and mighty" and the French cherishing the phrase "If it isn't clear, it isn't French."

But down on the ground, Russian is a language that hasn't bothered to grammaticalize a future marker. French has grammaticalized its *the* word into usage that no foreigner has ever found "clear"—to ask "I'd like water, please," you have to come up with "I'd like of the water"(?!?!??!). English has grammaticalized *have* into a present perfect construction (*Elvis has left the building*) that conveys a shade of difference from the simple past (*Elvis left the building*) that a great many foreign learners find "perfectly" unnecessary to communication! There are simply no grounds for judging one's own language to have grammaticalized the "right" way, or for which language has grammaticalized things "better." The lesson is simply that in any language, a word does not just stay the way it is, and one way it changes is to become a piece of grammar—sometimes a grammar word, sometimes a prefix or suffix or other kind of hiccup that is no longer a word at all.

And then, there's more change, because sounds are always changing along with meanings. "God is great, God is good, let us thank him for our food"—one can't help noticing that *good* and *food* don't rhyme, and it seems unlikely that the composers of such a solemn verse would have resorted to mere eye rhyming on the page. Or, "Jack and Jill went up the hill to fetch a pail of water / Jack fell down and broke his crown, and Jill came tumbling . . . . after." Is that the best they could do?

Of course not—and we'll learn in the next chapter why these things are the way they are.

4

A Vowel Is a Process

Words Start Sounding Different

I lived in upstate New York for a spell. One of the things that most strikes outsiders there is what is often called the region's "flat" *a*. *Cat* sounds more like what one might most readily transcribe as "kay-it," but that overshoots the reality. "Kay-it" sounds like a bad imitation of a southern drawl, and a common alternate attempt, "kyet," looks like something in Russian. It's more like "keh-it"—truthfully, somewhere in between "kay-it" and "keh-it." In any case, as an American you may well have heard this kind of pronunciation of what is often termed the "short" *a*. Indeed, it's not just with the word *cat* or any other mere set of words; it's that sound in general: *flat* is "fleh-it," *rabbit* is "reh-ihbit."

Alone, what's *that* all about? But it actually makes perfect sense.

— — —

An in-group epithet that young women of a certain demo-graphic have been using in the 2010s is *betch*, a transforma-tion of the word *bitch*. The Betches Like This website is an articulate demonstration of a tongue-in-cheek archetype, tartly defined in one source as "a well-groomed party girl who is smart enough to mock her vapid, privileged lifestyle but spoiled enough to endorse it at the same time." One sus-pects that the epithet will ultimately go down as a passing sign of an era in the way that *yuppie* and *preppie* did, but it still yields a question: why *betch*?

Alone, what's *that* all about? But it actually makes perfect sense.

I once spent a fair amount of time with a couple whose names were Dawn and Sean, and a friend of theirs named Ron. To me, Dawn and Sean's names rhymed, and then mine and Ron's did. But to most people in California, where we were, all four of our names rhymed. They pronounced Dawn as "Dahn" and Sean as "Shahn," such that we were "Dahn, Shahn, Jahn, and Rahn." This wasn't unusual: across the country, increasing numbers of people are pronouncing *aw* as *ah*.

Alone, what's *that* all about? But it actually makes perfect sense.

— — —

The sense in all these things becomes clear when we know two things: one, that English spelling is a tragic accident that steers us away from what's happening in our own mouths, and two, that vowels, like the meanings of words, are ever on the move. Not only a word but a sound is something going on rather than something that is.

But spelling sits at the gates of understanding like Cerberus, barring us from the fruits of enlightenment. We must first get past him.

Spelling: A Block on Perception

It is gruesome how much of an impediment English spelling is to internalizing the realities here. To learn how sounds work, we are cursed with having to divorce ourselves from how letters work. That's tough (think about how goofy the spelling of *tough* is!). We can't help thinking that letters are sounds, after all, just as we can't help thinking that Social Security is a matter of getting back money that we paid in. But ladies and gentlemen, letters are not sounds in any way that can help us, beyond the rickety purchase they gave us on learning how to spell—and most of us barely remember how that even worked.

We all know that English spelling is tricky and often irregular, but things are even worse than that. It's bad enough that we write the first sound in *thin* as *th*, when the actual sound is hardly a *t* with an *h* after it—do you say "tuh-HIN" for *thin*? However, it's even worse that the *th* in *thin* is a different sound from the *th* in *this*. Try the two out in your mouth to see what I mean. And yet we have no way of indicating that difference with letters. English letters are not English sounds.

As such, the way we have to write vowels is just a mess. The vowel is the same sound in all these words:

> free
>
> these
>
> leaf
>
> field
>
> seize
>
> key
>
> machine

but not in these:

> tough
>
> cough
>
> through
>
> thorough
>
> bough

Then, there are only five letters to indicate about a dozen different vowel sounds. The *u* stands for three different sounds in *cute*, *cut*, and *put*.

It is clear, then, that we must shift gears and think about sounds rather than letters to make sense of things, despite how vivid the letters are in our minds. Sadly, even the traditional notion of "long" and "short" vowels can take us only so far. Long *u*: *cute*. Short *u*: *cut*. Okay, but what's the sound in *foot*? Or *paw*? The *aw* is two letters but one sound. Long, short . . . what? We need help.

Bees in Your Mouth

A handy way to see what sounds, rather than letters, are like is with words that are the same in everything but the vowel (and not the letter but the actual sound) and then situate those words in our mouths. Why? Not just to make a chart like a third-grader doing a science report to show that he is diligent, tidy, and submissive. Only when we feel the vowels in our mouths do things like "keh-it," *betch*, and "Dahn, Shahn, Jahn, and Rahn" transform from weirdnesses to, as it were, ABC.

Let's start with *beet*, *bait*, and *bat*. They seem to have not a thing to do with one another—certainly not the concepts, but not even the sounds. They look out of order because we're used to the alphabet song. But in the grand scheme of things, the relationship of the alphabet song to English sounds is equivalent to the one between the castle in *Frozen* and the hundreds of small pieces of the Lego set of the castle in *Frozen* spread out on the floor.

Say *beet*, *bait*, and *bat* to yourself and you'll notice that you make all the vowel sounds in the front of your mouth. If that doesn't quite strike you yet, then say *bat* and then say *baht* (Thailand's currency) and notice that you have to pull backward for *baht*. That's the way that *beet* and *bait* and *bat* are up front.

Now, you can also feel that the vowel sound for *bait* is made lower than *beet*, and *bat* is made even lower than *bait*. Thus the sounds in *beet, bait*, and *bat* are a stack in the front of your mouth. Notice that the letters don't matter at all here. The vowels in *bait* and *bat* are written with the same letter *a*. *Beet* could be spelled *beat*. This is about sounds only. Here's what the sounds look like in terms of where they sit in your mouth:

beet

bait

bat

Let's do three more words: start with that *baht*. And then, think of *boat* and *boot*. *Boot*, *boat*, and *baht* stack up in the back of your mouth, right across from *beet*, *bait*, and *bat* up front. Just as *baht* is *bat* pulled back, you pull back from *bait* to say *boat*, and you pull back from *beet* to say *boot*. So the front stack is "ee," "ay," and ?—note that there is no way to even reliably spell the *a* sound in *bat*—and the back stack is "oo," "oh," and "ah."

beet	boot
bait	boat
bat	baht

But these vowels alone, if you think about it, don't get us what English sounds like. Apart from the *bat* sound, these are the vowels (ah, ay, ee, oh, oo) we associate with languages like Italian, of the kind that lend themselves well to opera singing. But if you give somebody a *tip*, which of these sounds are you using? The closest thing would seem to be "teep," but that sounds like English with an accent. We're missing the proper sound, and others.

Namely, most of the vowels we have already situated have a "friend" who is like them but different, different enough to be another sound entirely. Take *beet* and *bait*, for example. One need not go from *beet* immediately to *bait* in the way that you go from A to B—there's room in between. Think, say, of *bit*. Roll *bit* around and you can feel that in terms of how high it is in your mouth, it's like *beet* except a little lower down, and also pulled a touch farther back. Here, then, is the sound in *tip*, and we need to get that in:

beet	boot
bit	
bait	boat
bat	baht

But *bit* isn't just an isolated thing. Down below, you get the same thing between *bait* and *bat*. That is, what about not *ay*, but *eh*? There's *bait* but also *bet*—those are different sounds. And *bet* exists in the same relation to *bait* as *bit* to *beat*—a little farther down and a tad farther back. Like so:

beet	**boot**
bit	
bait	**boat**
bet	
bat	**baht**

Now, in line with the tidy opposition between the front stack of *beet*, *bait*, and *bat* and the back one of *boot*, *boat*, and *baht*, you get the same alternate duo in the back. Between *boot* and *boat* sits *book**—*book* is a little lower in your mouth, and also a bit more to the front than *boot* and *boat*. It fits in right across from *bit*:

beet	**boot**
bit	**book**
bait	**boat**
bet	
bat	**baht**

---

* Yes, I have to cheat a little here, because there happens to be no word that starts with a *b* and ends in a *t* with the vowel sound of *foot*, *put*, and *wood*. There is, in general, no series of words that all begin with the same consonant and end with some same other one that includes every single one of the possible vowels in between. For example, if I started with *peat* and *pat* and *pot*, then for the *oh* vowel I'd have to use an obscure British dialect word for kick, *pote*, and for *oo* I'd have to use *poot*, which frankly would get old.

Then, what happens here is a perfect example of why spelling "can't jump," so to speak. Yes, there indeed is a vowel between *boat* and *baht* that is lower than *boat* and pulled farther to the front. But it isn't spelled with a single letter. If we weren't so snookered by spelling, it would be easy to glean what that vowel was, but reality requires me to just lay it out: *bought*. Or, in an alternate universe I would prefer that *bought* were spelled "bawt"—it's the sound we most readily associate with *aw*. We put it here:

beet			boot
	bit	book	
bait			boot
	bet	bought	
bat			baht

With that, we have a nice parallel two "internal" stacks of vowels. Along with the *a* in *cat*, the *ih*, the *eh*, the *oo* in *book* ("eugh"?), and *aw* are, for better or for worse, what make English sound like English instead of Italian.

Except we're missing one last one: what you may have learned as "short" *u*, the vowel in *bus* and *but*. Where does that one go? (To see how misleading spelling is when it comes to vowels, note that this *uh* sound is the vowel in no fewer than three words I've just used—*but*, *does*, and *one*—despite the fact that only one of the words spells it with a *u*.) The *uh* sound is pronounced between the front stack and the back stack. Also, *but* is pronounced not as high up as *beet* and *boot*, but not as low down as *bat* and *baht*. Say *bait*, *but*, and then *boat* and you feel words pulling backward in an almost soothing straight line. This shows that *uh* goes smack in the middle, between front and back and between the top and the bottom:

beet		boot
bit		book
bait	but	boat
bet		bought
bat		baht

Here, then, is what and where our vowels are. Some readers may be waiting for the official phonetic symbols for the vowel sounds, intuiting that in a linguistics class we would be on our way to learning the International Phonetic Alphabet. However, for our purposes in this chapter, those symbols belong in the notes (where you will find them). Our interest is not in learning how to transcribe speech the way Henry Higgins in *Pygmalion* does, but in something simpler: internalizing a sense of how vowels sit in our mouths, in order to see the coherence in the different ways people pronounce words. For that, we just need something that takes us fleetly from the page to how we talk.

No, Not "Bees in Your Mouth"
Just Because Those Words in the Chart Begin with *B*

The next thing to understand is that the diagrams we have seen are, like dictionaries, snapshots of something that never stays the same. In an illustration of an atom, we understand that the electrons shown surrounding the nucleus do not, in reality, sit frozen in those positions. The electrons whiz around the nucleus. In the same way, a vowel is something going on, not a thing situated. To be a vowel is to face a future, maybe sooner, maybe later, but sometime, of becoming another vowel.

The diagram format obscures not only this, but the very nature of the environment the vowels have for this motility. The diagram implies "places" for the vowels, whereas in actuality vowels occupy an open field: your mouth. A vowel can pass through (note I did not write "sit") anywhere on that field. Each language's vowels consist of a mere fraction of the endless possibilities, and where a given vowel is pronounced in a given language at a given time is as much a matter of chance as what the temperature happens to be in Seattle right now, or exactly how many episodes of *The Simpsons* there will finally be. For example, there is no self-standing reason that the *oh* sound has to be exactly where Americans pronounce it, as if vowels fall into set places like marbles on a Chinese checkers board. Because there is no tin honeycomb of boxes in your mouth—if there is, do seek medical attention immediately—a vowel can be anywhere. There are many ways to be an *oh*.

Even within American English, *oh* is hardly in one place.

Take *boat* again: most Americans really say "boh-oot." It's Minnesotans who are famous for actually saying "boht," with what really is a simple "oh" sound. Then, many Philadelphians and Baltimoreans say something more like "beh-oot," where the sound is moving forward, toward the *bet* sound across from it. Many black Americans say something more like "baw-oot." So what is the "real" *oh* sound? That's just it—there's no such thing. For example, the most common American pronunciation, "boh-oot," is in no way basic, central, easier, or even earlier: for whatever it's worth, Old English speakers would have found Minnesotans' "boht" version the familiar one.

The takeaway is that a vowel is a moving thing, not a thing that is. These critters are alive, like bees in a hive. Any *oh* we hear today is where speakers of that language—or actually, speakers of that dialect of that language—happen to have alit at that time. Vowels exist in a field with no boundaries, such that they are not blocked in any way from moving—and they do.

More to the point, they *couldn't* sit still. The reason they move is that new generations tend to reproduce what they hear with a bit of distortion. People are imperfect mimics. "Oh-oo" happens because *oo* is a sound that happens on the way to passing from *oh* to somewhere else, or even to silence—*oh* requires a kissy pose with the lips, and *oo* is that same pose with lips a little closer to closed. A generation might start riding on that little *oo* a bit; the next generation, more, and the next thing you know, "boht" has become "boh-oot." Elsewhere, as speech flies out of your mouth you might not pull your *oh* back as far as Mom and Dad did—your *boat* starts to take on a redolence of the *bet* in front of it. After some generations, "boh-oot" has become "beh-oot."

There is a temptation to imagine that this vowel drift happens because of some kind of external influence, such as contact between people who speak in different ways. There is truth there. When different groups each lay their *oh* in different places, they may start affecting one another's placement of the vowel, and then more distortion happens when a new generation of people hear all these different renditions and settle on some kind of compromise. Contact between people does make a language change more quickly than normally.

However, external interventions like this are by no means a necessary condition for a language's changing, such as its vowels drifting. The change is, in itself, a default condition just as it is for weather. Contact between people speaking different languages, or dialects, only makes the vowels move in different directions *than they would have moved otherwise*—that is, the vowels would drift even among those people stuck in a cave. People born in there, in the dark waving bats away, would still render their parents' vowels somewhat inaccurately, adding bits here, clipping bits there, scooching things around a bit.

However, vowels do not jump willy-nilly from one end of the field to the other. They move in orderly fashion, one step at a time, just like the meanings of words. Once you have a sense of where the vowels are on the field—as opposed to an arbitrary row of symbols like *A E I O U*—then what strike us as peculiar accents end up seeming as ordinary as the fact that the long hand on the clock is in a different place

now than it was fifteen minutes ago. After all, why would it
not have moved?

Vowel Shifts Are What That's All About

Back to upstate New York. Why "keh-it" instead of *cat*? Or,
let's change it to "beh-it" for *bat*, to relate most directly to
our chart. As you can see, *bet* is just a step up from *bat*. The
bat vowel moved, as vowels will. Specifically, it floated up
to where *bet* is—not way up to where *beet* is, or up over to
where *but* is. In chess terms, vowels are kings, not rooks and
certainly not queens. To pronounce *bat* as "beh-it" isn't even
as eccentric as it may seem. If you are American and don't
happen to be in the group with this "flat" *a*, then say *cat* and
now say *man*. Do you really say *man* with the exact same
vowel as you say *cat* with? Some people do, but to most of
us it sounds a little odd or at least British. Most likely, you
say *man* in what you might think of as a "flatter" way—you
"squeeze" that *a* a bit when you say *man* (or *can*, or *ma'am*,
or *spam*, or *damn*). You're saying something more like "meh-
in." If this describes you, you do the squeeze before *m*'s and
n's. Other people just do it before all consonants—hence
"keh-it," plus "keh-ip" for *cap*, "peh-ik" for *pack*, and beyond.
You could even think of them as more consistent than the
rest of us!

The chess analogy continues: when *bat* moved up, it left
an empty space, ripe for something from nearby to come fill
it in. Something did: *baht* from right next door. This is why
the same woman who says "beh-it" may very well also

sound almost like she's saying "black" when she says *block*. Or this explains why some Americans will talk about the importance of what sounds like "jabs" rather than *jobs*. In real life we hear "jabs" as a "nasal" way of saying *jobs*. But someone speaking with these vowel shifts isn't talking any more through their nose than the rest of us. What's different between them and us is simply that their vowels are in different places from ours. "Jabs" is just *jobs* said in the forward part of your mouth, as in moving *baht* to *bat*. Someone whose vowels have moved in this particular way sounds almost like they're saying "the keh-it on the black" when they say "the cat on the block."

People's vowels have moved in this particular way in a swatch of the northern part of America's eastern half, which is why one hears it in upstate New York towns such as Buffalo and Rochester (it was Ithaca for me). It is also well established in Connecticut, and stretches westward to Cleveland, Chicago, Milwaukee, and most of Minnesota. It's called the Northern Cities Shift, and the way people in those places say *cat* and *flat*, although what sticks out most to the passing observer is but a taste of something larger and, in its way, elegant.

The vowels follow each other and get out of one another's way in a pleasantly choo-choo train fashion. Once the *baht* slot is empty because a person is saying *block* as "black," then up above that *baht* slot is *bought*, and indeed, people with this vowel shift also often pronounce *bought* more like *baht*, *caught* more like *cot*. This is all like a little train, you can see. So if *bat*, pulling along *baht* and *bought* behind it, has elbowed *bet* out of its area, then what happens to *bet* up front?

Well, the clockwise creep continues: *bet* ticks back into the area of *but*. If you know someone from the Northern Cities Shift region, watch them speaking and you might notice that they say a word like *bet*, *set*, or *met* in a way that will seem in passing as if they are opening their mouths a little wider. But actually, they are pulling the sound backward—a foreigner with no idea of what English looks like on the page, having met no one but a person with these vowels, might think a person saying *bet* was saying *but*, or at least sounded like they were. To this foreigner, the sentence *I'll bet she caught that cat down the block* would sound like something close to "I'll but she cot that kyet down the black." If you're not from the Northern Cities Shift region and you can render that sentence without exaggeration, just taking it light and saying it with neutral affect like someone saying it sitting on some front steps one July afternoon, you may find a Milwaukee accent in your mouth that you never expected.

This is not, however, an indication of anything odd about northern cities in the United States. It's just the way vowels happen to have been moving there. Everywhere else, they are moving, too—just in different ways. Vowels are like bees. In a hive where the bees are not moving, a likely analysis is that they are not alive. Similarly, a language in which the vowels stayed the same would be a language spoken either by robots or by a people so demoniacally obsessed with keeping their vowels in place that they would have to devote all life's energy to that task—which would be, essentially, death anyway.

Is This Really How a Language *Changes*?

I tell you that vowels are inherently, even ardently, motile. But then I exemplify it with the accent of people in Rochester and Milwaukee. You may wonder: is this business of how people sound here and there really a sign of how a *whole language changes*? Aren't these little things just, well, mannerisms, tics, or, to put it in a cocktail hour way, just some random (ahem) crap?

It seems like it—our lives aren't long enough for us to see the whole picture. It can be hard to even perceive vowel shifts going on in the present. Vowel shifts are slow, incremental, and subtle. We likely catch a mere glimmer, such as "keh-it," and hear it as an isolated anomaly. Even the people undergoing the vowel shift often hear themselves as talking just like everyone else. The Detroiter who says "jab" for *job*, if played a recording of another Detroiter saying "jab" for *job*, most often hears someone saying *jab* just as people from outside the Northern Cities Shift area do. They don't think of themselves as people who say something more like "jab" than *job*. The difference is fine-grained, and writing exerts a powerful pull on how we hear language, even our own. Is calling a job a "jab" really the kind of thing that ushered English from *Beowulf* to Bellow?

Yes, and the handiest way to see it is, as it happens, what most sources use as an introduction to the whole topic of vowel shifting. It's hardly that other books on linguistics don't mention that vowels move. However, the traditional way of getting the point across is to describe a vowel shift that happened in the fifteenth and sixteenth centuries, which is called, in fact, the Great Vowel Shift.

I have refrained from opening with it, because when described alone, the Great Vowel Shift implies that vowel movements—I couldn't resist just once—are something unusual, a museum exhibit safely removed in the past rather than life as it always is. Yet it was merely one phase in an ongoing process of which the Northern Cities Shift is a latter-day continuation. It is useful in showing that vowel shifting is normal, in that it stands out in a way that the Northern Cities Shift doesn't—on paper.

Namely, English spelling is hideous in large part because it represents what English was like before the Great Vowel Shift happened. That neatly demonstrates that vowels really are as liquid as I am presenting, and that what happens to them can neither be said to "ruin" the language nor be dismissed as bubblegum static, since no one wishes we could go back to talking the way Chaucer did.

Here's what I mean. Why would any sane person write *mate* and pronounce it "mayt"? We're used to being taught that this is a "long" *a* and that the "silent" *e* is our clue to that. But clearly no one would design a system this way. If people in France and Spain and seemingly everywhere else on earth were writing the "ay" sound as *e*, what was the sense of instead bringing in an *a* and signaling that it, instead of *e*, is pronounced "ay," and by putting a "silent" *e* at the *end* of the word? Why *e*? Or why use any sound at all as *standing for absence* instead of, duh, not writing anything there? While understanding that customs differ across the ages, we can be quite sure no writerly caste decided on such nonsense as a writing system. Sure, some eccentric medieval scribe could have arbitrarily decided on such a system, but why on earth would it have been accepted across England?

When something makes that little sense, usually it was created amid conditions now past in which they did make sense. And indeed, time was that *mate* was actually pronounced the way one would expect: MAH-tay. The final *-ay*, unaccented, wore off over time just as the *-ther* in *brother* has worn off among men saluting each other such that guys of a certain demographic call each other "bruh" and one might call one's sister "sis"—that's easy. "Mahtay" became "maht." But why don't we just say "maht" today? Because likely the vowel moved, and this one did.

"Maht" exited stage left: to *mat*, upon which it was poised to then do what *bat* did in the northern cities of something called America seven centuries later—it floated up. This time, it alit not on the *bet* slot but on the *bait* one. That, then, is why *mate* is spelled the way it is—*mate* represents how the word was said two steps behind—"MAH-teh." Speech moved on; spelling stayed put.

beet	boot
bit	book
mate but	boat
bet	bought
bat	baht

Then, once words like *mate* were in the *bait* slot, what was in that slot got pushed up, to the *beet* slot. Here is why, for example, *meet* is spelled the way it is. We're so used to seeing *ee* as standing for the sound in *beat*, *seize*, etc. However, in any other language you've learned, *e* likely stands for *ay* or *eh*. Why is *ee* the vowel sound in *beet* just because there are two *e*'s? If *e* is *ay*, then shouldn't *ee* be, if anything, "ayy"?

Yes, and once, it was. *Meet* was once pronounced as it "should" be: "mate." The two *e*'s instead of one just meant that it was more like "ayy" than "ay," a difference which in earlier stages of English actually made the difference between one word and another. In Old English, if you said "may-tuh" it meant *meat*, while only by stretching it out into "mayy-tuh" could you mean *meet*.* But, edged out and above the *ay* slot, *meet* came to be pronounced the way it is now, but again, the spelling held on. So: *mate* and *meet* are both spelled crazily because of the Great Vowel Shift.

---

* This issue of vowel length is why the Great Vowel Shift involved two-step jumps, like pawns on their first move, rather than moving one slot at a time. This was a shift involving long vowels; the vowels in the inner ring of slots (clockwise, *book*, *bought*, *bet*, and *bit*) were not long. Vowel length seems a rather arcane thing to us now, because we don't use it to distinguish words. Imagine if "meeet" meant to make someone's acquaintance, while vegetarians were people who didn't eat "meet," said at a quick, beepy clip. I'm actually kind of glad we don't do that. But in earlier English, vowel length was that important, to the point that, for example, a vowel shift might single out just the long vowels while the short ones just hung out for a while (but only for a while!).

meet	boot
bit	book
mate	but	boat
bet	bought
bat	baht

The Great Vowel Shift was even beautiful, in the way that mathematicians and physicists often describe the workings of their solutions. Well, not quite that beautiful, but close. Over on the back row, wouldn't you know, *moose* is pronounced the way it is for the same reason *meet* across from it is pronounced the way it is. Again, *o* is supposed to indicate *oh*, and so *oo* should by all rights stand for two *ohs*, "ohh." That's how an early medieval English speaker thought of things as well: *moose* was pronounced "mohhs." One saw one of those oddly majestic creatures and said, "Look at that mohhs."

However, "mohhs" moved up to the *boot* slot in the same way that "mayyt" moved up to the *meet* slot over across, and thus "mohhs" became our *moose*:

meet		**moose**
bit		book
mate	but	boat
bet		bought
bat		baht

Then, finally, the Great Vowel Shift became a vowel *spill*, like out of a fountain. From both sides! If the pronunciation of "mayyt" moved it up to the *beet* slot, then where did what was already in the *beet* slot go? *Mite* was in it—pronounced, at first, "MEE-tay," just as it would be in any normal language where *i* stands for *ee*. If you have studied Spanish, imagine how *mite* would be pronounced in it: "MEE-tay." That's normal. Why, then, is *mite* in English today pronounced like *might*?

You'd never guess, but it made sense. Think of a southerner with a good solid drawl saying *meet*—it's more like "muh-eet." It isn't hard to start pronouncing a vowel with a little *uh* before it—note today how often younger people say "Wuh-it???" rather than "What?" From *meet* to "muh-eet" was the exact same pathway, for the same reason of articulatory serendipity. Little alternate ways of saying things, among the infinite array of ones possible, settle randomly in.

But look: in our chart, that little *uh* in "muh-eet," *uh* being the *but* sound, sits a step up from *ah* down on the lower right. Hence, over time "muh-eet" became "mah-eet"—that is, our *mite*. In terms of where it is pronounced in the mouth, the vowel in *mite* is neither fish nor fowl: one part *ah* and one part *ee*, it doesn't fit neatly above *beet* in any coherent way. Rather, *mite* just branched off in a little spew:

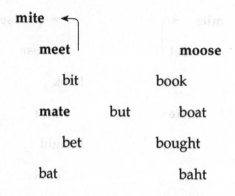

Then, what happened to *oo* when moved in on by words like "mohhs"? Same thing: the Old English rendition of *mouse* was in the *oo* slot, pronounced "moose." Now, a southern American transplanted to Merrie Olde England might pronounce it as "muh-oos" in his accent. As it happened, a Middle English speaker was given to saying it just that way. First "muh-oos," eventually a step southeast to "mah-oos," and that's *mouse*. (Then, many speakers move that *ah* in "mah-oos" over a notch leftward to the *bat* sound.) So what began as an imposing car-smashing horned *mose* and a squeaky little rodent *moose* became a horned *moose* and a squeaky little *mouse*. The vowel in *mouse* no more fits in above *boot* in our chart than *bite* fits in above *beet*, and so we can draw it in as a complementary spew on the right:

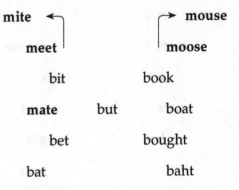

There was actually one last little afterpiece, which finally explains the *good/food* problem. Later on, some words that had wound up in the *boot* slot made another move, down left into the *book* slot. *Food*, as it happened, stayed put, but *good* moved to *book*—voilà, the ruin of what once rhymed in the famous prayer. Then some words like this moved even farther in, to the *but* slot—such as *blood* and *flood*. This is why, then, *food*, *good*, and *flood* don't rhyme. Hence also the trio *poot*, *put*, and *putt*—given that *u* in languages usually means the *oo* sound, we can see how all three of these words "should" be pronounced "poot," and they once were.

beet		**food**	
bit		**good**	
bait	**flood**		boat
bet		bought	
bat		baht	

All that was vowel shifting, of the exact same kind that makes a person in Detroit talk about getting a "jab." "Jab" looks somewhere between trivial and bemusing, but it is a modern symptom of what, occurring bit by bit and piling high, blocked us from being able to converse with Chaucer. The enshrinement of the Great Vowel Shift in the traditional story of the English language is like documenting the classical symphony of Mozart and Beethoven as the essence of Western music, as if Palestrina, Handel, and Bach were just preludes and Debussy, Schoenberg, Gershwin, and bebop were just footnotes. Just as music has always changed and we couldn't imagine that it wouldn't, vowels always shift and make words drift into new renditions of what they once temporarily were.

One Never Knows

The analogy with bees in the hive must be pushed further, to show how it applies to so much around us. For example, so far it may seem like vowel shifts are almost always clockwise for some reason. We've seen "mohhs" going counterclockwise to become *moose*, but seemingly only because the equivalent thing ("mate" becoming *meet* clockwise) was happening over on the other side. But the wheel goes both ways.

In Old English, dogs chewed on "bahns," it was sticks and "stahns" that broke your "bahns," and there was no place like "hahm." The *ah* sound rose, *counterclockwise*, and thus by Middle English the words were *bone*, *stone*, and *home*.

Or, there is also a vowel shift happening in California. The *bit* vowel has collapsed, *counterclockwise*, down into the *bet* space, such that someone saying *bit* sounds more like they are saying *bet*. The mental domination of the written word, plus context, ensures that when a young Californian says "a little bet" for *a little bit*, we do not mishear. However, if you know any such people, play a mental audio file of them saying "leave a tip" and note how their *ih* sound has a lot of *eh* in it. Or, imagine, if I may, them saying the word for a female dog, and we have the explanation for the "Betch" joke. The routine stems from California, and "betch" is how women below a certain age in that state actually say *bitch*. The California shift is a choo-choo train chain, too: if *bit* is in *bet*, then *bet* likely moves on, and it goes down to the *bat* slot. "Make the bed," a young or youngish someone from Santa Barbara says, and it sounds more like "Make the bad."

Thus vowel shifts can go either way, even at the same time. In California you have chains within chains, gears within gears within gears, shifting in opposite directions. People in California (and a ways eastward, especially Texas) often pronounce *pink* as "peenk" and *king* as "keeng." It can seem like a little oddity—I've seen it mocked—but in terms of our chart it's business as usual. *Pink* has the vowel in *bit*; "peenk" is the vowel in *beet*, just a step up. But wait—if this is California, why didn't *pink* become "penk" like *bit* became *bet*? Because *ng*, *n*, and *m* have a way of creating their own little dramas. They are the nasal consonants—the ones you can buzz on—and making them requires closing the mouth at least somewhat at the back. When you say a word, your brain has the whole word planned before it comes out, and when we say a vowel, we have a way of anticipating what the sound after it is going to make the tongue do. When an *m, n,* or *ng* is coming, that means anticipating the tongue lift, such that *pink* goes up, clockwise, to "peenk." And *man,* down below at *bat,* even comes up for the ride, to "mee-an"—the buzzing consonants can even pull that *bat* vowel all the way up to *beet.* When I did my graduate work in California, I noticed that people born there tended to say "mee-an" for *man* (and "stee-ind" for *stand,* "hee-um" for *ham,* and so on); linguistics taught me why.*

Vowels really are, then, like bees in a hive, bumbling all over the place. You never know just where a bee might wiggle off to—or if chaos theory experts can tell us, the explanation would likely somehow not feel quite like one. Say you're watching episodes of the old sitcom treat *The Many Loves of Dobie Gillis* (as all of us of course do from time to time) and in one of them the father character calls an orchid an "ar-chid," asks, "What is this used *far?*," and tells someone,

---

* Here, too, is what's up with the famous Wisconsin "bayg" for *bag.* It is all but impossible not to find it "cute" as an outsider, I openly admit. But it's also just a matter of "Oh, of course . . ." in terms of the vowel chart. The *bat* sound has moved up to the *bait* slot, pulled up there because of what *g* is like. The *ng* sound and *g* are both produced by hiking your tongue up in the back of the mouth; to anticipate making a *g* means lifting things up a bit. Naturally, then, *bag* becomes "bayg," to haggle is to Hegel, and so on. (Yes, I'm smiling. But then, I'm from Philadelphia and I say "woo-der" for *water,* which is not even part of something systematic like a vowel shift—it's just some one-off mess!)

"You're getting 'wahhrm'!" instead of "wore-m," as most of us say the word. It's a subtle thing, and so there's no way the actor, Frank Faylen, was directed to use *ar* for *or* in this way. Rather, this was the way Faylen happened to talk, and it's no accident that Faylen was from St. Louis. A peculiarity of pronunciation there is that, to quote the most cherished example, Highway 40 is pronounced "Highway Farty." On the *Gillis* show, Faylen called corn "carn," and so on.

But it's only so peculiar—the *ah* slot is just below the *aw* slot, and therefore "fawr-tee" to "farty" is a quick trip. Next time you're with someone from St. Louis, listen for it— although they can't be, well, young. The "wahrm archid" pronunciation is on its way out—it's shining bright in the elderly, more modest but steady in their kids, and all but nonexistent among young people. For example, on the sit-com *The Office* (U.S. version), both Phyllis Smith (as Phyllis) and Ellie Kemper (as Erin, and later well-known as Kimmy Schmidt) are St. Louisans. Smith (sixtyish at the time of the show) had the *ar* for *or*; Kemper (then thirtyish) did not.

But is this St. Louis "farty" thing weird? Only if we discount something happening across the nation. Take away the *r* in *for* and *far*, and the pronunciation of the vowels alone, *aw* and *ah*, is becoming the same for ever more people across America these days. As a linguistics teacher, I find it an ever-weirder challenge to teach what is becoming an ever-growing number of students in any class that, for some people, *cot* and *caught* do *not* rhyme. To me, *cot* is "caht" and *caught* is "cawt." But that's because I grew up in Philadel-phia. For people in the western half of the country and most of New England as well as among many people in the

Northern Cities Shift zone and more people elsewhere by the decade, both *cot* and *caught* are pronounced "caht."

Here, then, is why so many people spontaneously rhymed Dawn ("Dahn"), Sean ("Shahn"), John, and Ron. A vowel shift is happening, and has been for a long time. I recall taking issue with a girl in my elementary school class in the early seventies when we were talking about the television show *Maude*. (My mother made me watch it because it was educational about societal issues—and she just liked it—but yes, it is odd that I was talking about it with little Julie Pinchuk.) She pronounced it "Mod," and I kept saying, "No, it's Maww-d!" Either Julie or her parents were probably transplants from somewhere north or far west of Philadelphia, where this conversation took place. But Julie was a sign of the times: vowels shifting just as they had been during the Black Plague. They've never stopped.

Thus what seems vocally odd is just vowels making their chess moves, despite how culturally rooted the shifts can accidentally seem. Brooklynites in the old days were well known for having "oy" for "er," as in "toity-toid" for *thirty-third*. As a child I heard a glimmer of this from the last generation of young people to grow up with it—sometime in the early seventies, when my family took me on a trip to New York on the Fourth of July (I forget why), a kid of about nine or ten was on the sidewalk selling "Fire-woiks! Fire-woiks!" It didn't occur to me until much later, however, that my own older black southern relatives had the exact same pronunciation of such words—*shirt* was "shoit," *work* was indeed "woik." Louis Armstrong is probably the most recorded black person exhibiting this vowel shift. On recordings he made in his home he casually talks about how his horn comes "foist" and how he needs someone to keep his horn "poi-colatin'" (for *percolating*).

However, this was hardly unique to him, nor, as sometimes implied in sources about *oy* for *er*, only a trait of the New Orleans where Armstrong happened to have grown up. It was normal in the English of the Deep South in the old days. One catches it regularly in black performers born across the South in the early twentieth century,* cases in which one might wonder why they have "Brooklyn" accents when actually it was just that the bees happened to make the same move where they grew up as they did in Brooklyn. After all, a hive is only so big.

Then, finally, you never know how far those bees will skitter—they can stop shorter in some places than in others. For example, we saw how in what became Standard English, vowel-wise some words jumped from *boot* to *book* and then to *but*: what was once *blude* jumped two steps in to *bludd*. But in northern England and Scotland, words did not take the second step to the *but* slot, and instead just stayed *put* in the *put* slot. This is why people speaking those dialects say *but*, *love*, and *blood* with a vowel that rhymes with *book*

---

* But how is *er* to *oy* a chess move? It's spelling that makes it hard to see. Neither Brooklynites nor southern blacks ever actually said "woyk" for *work*. The sound was actually what happens when you do four quick things: (1) Say *work*; (2) now say *work* but stop before the -*rk*; (3) now repeat 2 but then add a little *ee* sound to the end; (4) now put a *k* on the end and you are speaking old Brooklyn (or old black Atlanta). In other words, the vowel in -*er* stayed the same; what changed was the *r*, into a little squeak. It happens.

instead of *but*. Most of us just hear it as quaint or as what is typical of the non-elite characters in *Game of Thrones*. But it's actually quite predictable from the layout of our grid, otherwise known as the human mouth.

Also, take the grand olde Scottish folk song "Annie Laurie"—a singer doing a savory rendition will end it with "I'd lay doon my head and dee" for *I'd lay down my head and die*. Why do the Scots say it "like that"? There's an easy reason—there was no "spew" in Scotland! In what became Standard English, *down* started as "doon" and then became "down" just as "moos" became *mouse* and "hoos" became *house*. But in Scotland, words like "doon" just stayed where they were—no spew into "down." And there was a systematicity to this, in that over in front, the words up in *ee* didn't spew into "aye," either. Just as our *bite* started as pronounced "beet," our *die* started as pronounced "dee." In Scotland it stayed that way—hence lying doon to dee. One never knows—at least one can't beforehand, but one can nevertheless understand afterward.

Oh, yes—what about Jack and Jill? Well, it's one more lesson in how sounds change in predictable ways that leave strange-looking results. You're British and you say AHF-ter. Said for eons, and often, as is a word like *after*, you can imagine that it could be shortened into AH-ter—which, note, rhymes just fine with *water*! In many dialects of English in Britain, *after* actually has long been "ah-ter," and "Jack and Jill" was written in one of those dialects. That doesn't really follow directly from the *particular* things I have discussed in this chapter, but I have always wanted to get this in somewhere, and you must admit it's fun to know.

How Should I Pronounce?

With vowels this restless even today, it follows that people even as recently as a hundred or so years ago would sound odd to us simply because their vowels, like their hair styles and hemlines, were in different places than ours today. We can in fact know this, from what people at the time confidently proclaimed as the "proper" way to pronounce words.

A perfect example was one William Henry P. Phyfe, an American specialist in pronunciation in the late nineteenth century, who made a career with books teaching people the "best" way to speak. Anyone who followed his advice in our times would be at a distinct social *dis*advantage, in pronouncing words in ways we would consider quite beyond consideration. Often it's because vowels can't stay put.

"Correct pronunciation," Phyfe assured us in the preface to one of his books, *How Should I Pronounce?*,

> is the best *prima-facie* evidence of general culture. On this account it appeals to all, since there is no one wholly indifferent to the estimate formed of his social position, and who, in consequence, would not cultivate those arts that are at once the criteria of social standing and the stepping-stones to a more liberal culture.

The man was serious. It would be too easy to mock him as a clueless social striver who didn't understand that language is inherently changeable, though. He actually understood this better than many of his equivalents of the era:

Some people, for instance, seem to think that the pronunciation of words never varies. Tell them that it is constantly
changing; that there are many words that are pronounced
in several different ways; that the question of correctness
in this matter is one wholly of custom;—and we unfold to
their minds a condition of things of which they before had
no conception.

Yet Phyfe's idea is that the way "cultivated" people happen
to be pronouncing words at his given moment is, for better
or for worse, what anyone who seeks their status (station?)
must imitate.

That means that Phyfe's little book allows us to listen in
on how the kinds of people in Edith Wharton novels were
pronouncing words in their drawing rooms, or at least the
way they thought they were supposed to be pronouncing
them. And, boy, would these people have sounded odd to
us! Phyfe provides a lengthy glossary of words to watch out
for, and we encounter one word after another for which he
crisply prescribes a pronunciation that today would have
people telling us we probably need to get more sleep.

Apparently there were people in 1885 pronouncing
daunt, haunt, and *taunt* as "dahnt," "hahnt," and "tahnt," and
Phyfe thinks of these as "correct." That people would pronounce these words that way is not surprising in itself, given
that, as we have seen, the *baht* vowel is just a step away from
the *bought* vowel that so many of us pronounce *daunt, haunt,*
and *taunt* with today. But Phyfe does not overall suggest
that all *aws* be pronounced as *ah,* as in today's California

(and elsewhere) accent, with *cot* for *caught*, *hock* for *hawk*, and *rah* for *raw*. That accent didn't exist in 1885. What Phyfe was advising was something much more specific: *aw* becoming *ah* before just *n*. As Gilded Age sophisticates, we were also to say "lahnch" for *launch*, "lahndry" for *laundry*, and of course, "ahnt" rather than "ant" for *aunt*. Then also, apparently, for consistency's sake, *can't* was to be pronounced "cahnt" like the name of the philosopher.

During the administrations of presidents like Chester Alan Arthur, Grover Cleveland, and Benjamin Harrison, then, the cultivated American might *correct* herself into saying "lahndry" instead of *laundry* and tell her children to do the same, and talk of "hahnted" houses. In 1885: music in different forms, clothing in different cuts, vowels in different slots. For Phyfe, *isolate* was "izzolate," *equable* was "ee-quable," *sacrilegious* was "sacriLEEjus," and *nomad* was "NAH-mad." A person of grace and substance just 125 years ago could say, in all seriousness, "It would be sacrileejus to izzolate those nahmads." Things change, for no real reason. Across the Atlantic, in France, about fifteen years after Phyfe published his book, two British academics were touring Versailles when, they claimed, they slipped into a time warp back to 1789. They later said they spoke to various people, including Marie Antoinette. You are not alone in finding this story unlikely; the two women were politely ridiculed for years after they wrote a book on the subject. However, there is one thing in their account that does ring true: they mentioned that the French they heard was oddly pronounced. Not just "olde" in terms of vocabulary and grammar (although they mentioned that, too), but because people sounded funny. That detail isn't something most people, academics or not, would know to include in an account like theirs about just a century-and-change before. "Funny" is exactly how the French of 1789 would sound to modern speakers, because sounds ooze around—*a*'s then weren't quite like *a*'s now, etc. We can know the same thing about American English at the same remove from us as 1789 was from those professors, with a look at books like Phyfe's.

Consonants get jostled around as a language moves along, too, and Phyfe's American English demonstrates this amply. As with vowels, consonants don't differ in random ways; what Phyfe wants is always a close cousin of the consonant we use today, such as soft versions of consonants for which we are accustomed to the hard versions.* *Dishonest* is to be pronounced "diz-honest," *suffice* "suffize," and *Greenwich* "grinage." Now and then Phyfe shows us, in what he shoos away, things that are just plain odd. At *girl*, he advises, "Do not introduce a y sound before the 'i' in this word. It is regarded as an affectation." Of course, today, none of us need be told not to say "gyirl." Who would? Phyfe's comment shows that in 1885 there were people *actually going around saying "gyirl" and thinking of it as classy!* Who knew?

Phyfe is also valuable in showing something else about how words sound from one era to another. A witticism that gets around is the idea of someone "putting the em-PHA-sis on the wrong syl-LA-ble." In fact, if we traveled to even the recent-ish past and listened around, we would hear a considerable degree of just that.

---

* Linguists, actors, et al.: yes, I mean voiced versus voiceless consonants.

For example, in the mid-nineteenth century, the English poet Samuel Rogers commented in his recollections, "The now fashionable pronunciation of several words is to me at least very offensive: CON-template—is bad enough; but BAL-cony makes me sick." To Rogers, the normal way of saying those words was con-TEM-plate and bal-CO-ny.* Yet this is not someone living in the Middle Ages; he lived long enough to be photographed!

As did Phyfe, and he, too, thought of con-TEM-plate as a normal way to say that word, but that's only the beginning. For Phyfe, a melodrama was a melo-DRA-ma, an inquiry was an in-QUI-ry, one il-LUS-trated things, and some matters took pre-SEED-ence over others. A gaslight-era Daffy Duck would have called Bugs Bunny DEHS-pi-kuh-bul (that one is my favorite), and if the cartoon were about the two of them as soldiers, Daffy's umbrage would perhaps be for Bugs having woken him up before not REH-vul-ee but ree-VALE-yay. Dogs were kay-NINE, not KAY-nine, and in Phyfe's world, one valued things like a BUFF-ett (not a buh-FAY) for being EX-emplary and EX-quisite, and might com-PEN-sate for one's original sin via ce-LIB-acy, being HOS-pitable, or giving somebody a nice, juicy "NEC-tarin." Oh yes: Phyfe also wanted us to always remember to pro-nounce *nucleolus* "nu-CLE-olus" rather than the slangy "nucle-O-lus" that we are all so accustomed to tossing off.

In Jack Finney's sci-fi romance *Time and Again*, in which

---

* Rogers actually used accent marks over the vowel of the accented syllable; i.e., cóntemplate. I am using capital letters for uniformity with the other transcriptions of accent in this section.

the protagonist goes back to 1882 and meets the love of his life, one of the things he and Julia would have bantered about would have been her casually pronouncing words with these accents, having been taught by schoolmarms and relatives that this was the proper way to say them. Yet, ultimately, banter is all their exchanges on this topic could have qualified as. There is no metric to determine which is the right or wrong way to accent a word from era to era. Words' accents can vary arbitrarily in the same way as where their vowels sit. The accent can rock from syllable to syllable in a word over time, rather the way the magnetic poles of the earth switch endlessly back and forth.

Or, at least, it's often random in that way. However, there are times when the accent moving is part of a new word's being born. It's happening all the time, and yet we are no more aware of it than we are of ultraviolet light. For example, did you ever think about the fact that you re-CORD a REC-ord? It looks like that difference in accent is an accident—but it isn't.

5

Lexical Springtime

Words Mate and Reproduce

You can't keep them apart. Words, that is. You can try, with your spaces between them—but wait, that's only on paper. We don't speak spaces. Just say that last sentence and notice that you uttered no spaces. One word comes immediately on the tail of the other one. The Ancient Greeks didn't even bother to indicate spaces when they wrote, and in that, their writing reflected speech more accurately than modern writing conventions do, despite what a pain it was to read such text.

When things are pushed up against one another they have a way of sharing and blending, as we know from stew, the history of jazz, and dormitories. Words are similar: something else that can happen to a word is that it can join with another one to create a new word entirely.

We have seen in chapter 3 how if a word becomes a piece of grammar it may stick to another word and become a prefix or suffix. But when that happens, the root word is still standing, modified only by a new bit of material. *Walked* is just a version of *walk*, not a new word; *entire* and *entirely* exist in the same relationship.

But at other times, the result is neither a version of one word or the other, but something brand new. Part of what makes a language alive is that new words come not only from people making up new words for new things, or taking words from other languages, but from words mating and yielding new ones.

Hangry for Brunch?

That in itself may not seem like news. We are all familiar with cute coinages like *sitcom* from *situation comedy*, *motel* from *motor hotel*, and *camcorder* from *camera recorder*. Linguists call these *blends*: *smog* (smoke, fog), *electrocute* (electric, execute), and *brunch* (breakfast, lunch) are further examples, and blending created many ancient words for which we'd never suspect anything amiss in their history. Words involving sounds and movement seem to have been especially susceptible to yielding blends: *flush* is apparently what happened when *flash* met *gush*, and if given a second to think about it, one can almost guess that *twirling* is *twisting* plus *whirling*.

Modernity has increased the chances of such words

catching on. Blends initially have an air of levity or artifice, of a kind one might expect only a small set of people to embrace as a kind of in-joke. However, the modern media create an artificial sense of community over broader spaces and exert endless repetition. This makes it more likely that words like *palimony* and *staycation* acquire a certain purchase.

Only a certain purchase, however. The smile that blends like the previously mentioned ones elicit is a sign that such words often never quite shake an air of being mannered, as often as not generated by Madison Avenue. In an episode of Lucille Ball's second sitcom *The Lucy Show*, she offers her maid what is supposed to be a special lunch, saying, "It's broasted." I wondered what that meant when seeing the episode in reruns in the seventies, have asked various people since who always draw a blank, and have been bemused to catch it mentioned as a new coinage in a book about English from precisely the year that episode first aired. Created in reference to things of the moment, blends have a way of falling away once that moment is past. For every *chortle* (Lewis Carroll pulled that one in his poem "Jabberwocky") there is a *cafetorium*, the sort of item whose listing as an official word stays viscerally perplexing to more than a few.

A delightful blend getting around as I write this is *hangry*, describing someone in a bad mood because they're hungry. But is this, an artifice wrought by deliberate human interference, what we want to learn about when examining the life history of words and where they come from? In a class on evolution, we'd be disappointed if the professor spent three weeks on the cloning of Dolly the sheep. One of mature thought's eternal challenges is figuring out where to draw the proverbial line, and there is no real answer here as to what consititutes a "real word." However, things like *hangry* and *manny* (a male nanny) carry a definite whiff of being more new jokes than new words, although one never knows what may just settle in for real.

What's the Nilly in *Willy-Nilly*?

To really get at a process that generates many more new words than blending does, in a way organic rather than crafted, and also less obvious and therefore more interesting, we need to start elsewhere. Such as with the fact that there are always perfectly humble words that combine a pair of meanings. There always have been. Example: in earlier English, the way you made a sentence negative was to put *ne* before it. In Old English, *I have* was *ic hæbbe*. *I don't have* was *ic ne hæbbe*. It was pretty simple, much like the way you make a sentence negative in most languages: you put something like *no* before the verb. Only later in English did we start putting *do* before the verb and inserting *not* before it.*

---

* The reason for the *do* was actually rather interesting: languages like Welsh use *do* this way, and when speakers of such languages switched to the English of the invading Angles, Jutes, and Co., they spoke English "in Welsh," as it were, and there were more of them than there were of anybody

Anyway, because *ne* was a short little word uttered an awful lot, people had a way of running it onto the words that came after it. The result was a bunch of fun combination words in Old and Middle English. In Old English, to say *I don't have the book*, you said "I nave the book," with the *nave* resulting from *ne* and *have* mashed together. (Actually, *næbbe*, but I am "translating" into the modern form for clarity.) Well into Middle English, these kinds of contractions were everywhere. One must get used to them to read Chaucer in the original, beyond the famous opening lines of *The Canterbury Tales*, which are fortuitously easier to understand as a Modern English speaker than most of Chaucer's language.

"Ther daweth me no day," he writes in his poem *The Legend of Good Women* "that I nam up and walkyng in the mede." That meant: There dawns me no day that I *am not* (*ne+am=nam*) up and walking. *I am not* was *nam*, *is not* was *nis*, *were not* was *nere*. If I'm speaking Middle English, if I want to, *I will*, but if I don't want to, I *nill*. There were even contractions like this for *know*—except the verb was different. *He knows* was *he woot*. So, *he doesn't know* was *he noot*!

This is the kind of thing that you might wish English still had. We do, actually. For one, in *willy-nilly*, the *nilly* is straight from the old *nill*. Also, *none* is from *ne* and *one*, and *never* is from *ne* and *ever*. But those may not feel like the same thing. Since we don't have *ne* alone anymore, *none* and

---

else. The rest was history. I describe this process in greater detail in my book *Our Magnificent Bastard Tongue* (New York: Gotham Books, 2008).

never don't feel to us as if they start with a *ne*. And *willy-nilly* is an isolated and slightly twee expression, unaccompanied by a hypothetical set of others like "havey-navey" or an "Is-nis!" perhaps said with a dismissive shrug along the lines of "Taxes, schmaxes!"

However, as English lost the old forms, it gained new ones, in the form of what we traditionally call contractions. They arose starting in the early 1500s, having begun in less crunched forms such as *donnot* for *don't* and *wonnot* for *won't*, of which *cannot* has for some reason held on despite *can't* existing alongside. We no longer have *nis* from *ne+is*, but we have *isn't*, and while *nave* is no more, we have *haven't*. The apostrophes do not make *isn't* and *haven't* different from *nis* and *nave*. The apostrophe is not pronounced; nor does it mark a pause: it is simply a convention of how we transcribe speech into marks on a page, and quite an arbitrary one: comprehension would suffer not a bit if we wrote *isnt* and *hasnt*. Or, if the dice had landed differently and apostrophes had been invented earlier, in Middle English *nis* would have been *n'is*, *nill n'ill*, etc. Rather, *isn't* is, in its unwritten essence, an utterance "isunt," different no more or less from "is-not" than *nis* was from "ne-is."

If *isn't* and *haven't* still don't feel quite as "smushed" as words like *nill*, then consider *won't*—there is no conceivable "wo" word that the *n't* follows. *Won't* is a pleasantly unpredictable mating of *will* and *not*, with traits from both but an individuality all its own. *Don't* is similar in terms of how it is pronounced. Why not "doont"? We don't pronounce *do* as "dough." And let's not even get into *ain't*. "Ai-not?" That's the most eccentric of the contractions, and wouldn't you know, those who dare true peculiarity are banned from general society.

Yet, in the end, forms like *nill* and *don't* and *ain't* still strain the notion of "new word." Even if their shape has gone beyond what the parent words' shapes were, they retain the two meanings—they are two words in one package. *Won't* doesn't sound like what happens if you mash *will* and *not* together, but its meaning is still that of *will* and *not*. Linguists call these, in fact, portmanteau forms—they are like bags you carry more than one thing in. It can be more than two—consider *wouldn't've*, remembering that we don't pronounce apostrophes! But still, you could take each piece out of the bag by itself.

But words can mix harder than that. Imagine reaching into the bag and finding purée—except that it's frozen into the shape of a new . . . well, that analogy hits a wall, but you'll see what I mean.

The Usual Sus-PECTS

In the 1934 film *The Thin Man*, as in all the films in its series, eventually detective Nick Charles gathers together all the people connected to a crime case he's been unraveling. However, if you listen closely, there's something a little odd about how William Powell (as Nick) delivers one of his lines: he talks about gathering together not the "SUS-pects," but the "sus-PECTS."

It's the kind of thing that leads one to ask: *why* did he say it that way? But the real answer is a broad one, not something about the word *suspects*, or William Powell, or the old days. It isn't, for example, that Powell was trying to sound British: Nick and Nora Charles are elegant indeed, but very much Americans. Part of their charm is in conveying the aristocracy that they do while at the same time being so very red, white, and blue with their easygoing banter and martinis.

The actual reason is, of all things, central to the birth of new words. However, to get at the matter properly requires starting from what will seem oddly far away from an evening watching *The Thin Man*. It's something one never has occasion to think about. When it's brought to your attention, it seems as dull as that earnest person you want to run from at a party. But bear with me: you sus-PECT someone of doing something, upon which they are a SUS-pect. Notice: you would never say you SUS-pect someone of something. Why? Because SUS-pect, with the accent on the first syllable, is the way you say it when using it as a noun. Put another way, the fact that the accent is on the first syllable is what *makes* SUS-pect a noun, in the same way that other words are made into nouns by tacking on a suffix, like -*ness* in *happiness*.

In 1934, however, *suspect* had yet to fully make the transition from being only a verb (*I suspect you of lying*) to having a noun form alongside (gathering the *suspects*). Things tend to take time, and typically, between A and B there is a stage when things are neither completely A nor B but something in between: the teenager, Jell-O when you can still stir it but only slowly, or gathering the sus-PECTS. There was a time when saying SUS-pects for the noun was common, but you could still say sus-PECTS without being asked what was wrong with you. This is why Powell was saying sus-PECTS in 1934, whereas eight years later, in *Casablanca*, Claude Rains said, "Round up the usual SUS-pects."

Who *cares* about this word? Nobody, in itself—but it's an example of something general. When a verb becomes a noun in English, if it has two syllables, something happens very quietly, so quietly that I have never known anyone who noticed it by themselves. The accent shifts backward. It's why someone who re-BELS is a REB-el, whose crimes you can re-CORD and thereby leave them on REC-ord for all to see. It's why your tooth may be im-PACT-ed and have a negative IM-pact on your sense of well-being.

Let's pull the camera back some now. The shift of the accent backward—from now on we'll call it the Backshift—is much more widespread than just in verbs becoming nouns. Someone from 1950 noticing that we send photos as digital files would be missing the picture, so to speak, if they stopped at marveling that we can do only that, as opposed to also sharing live conversation, written messages, and music in the same way. Similarly, the Backshift is not only a secret way to make a new noun; it's a secret way to make a new word in general. It is how a way of expressing something in our language becomes "a thing" as opposed to a one-off or a passing peculiarity.

More to the point: the Backshift doesn't happen only to single words; it happens to pairs of them, and knits them together in the process. An example is the difference between *black board* and *blackboard*. A black board is some board that someone painted black. A blackboard is the particular thing made of slate that hangs on a schoolroom wall. *Black board* is pronounced "black BOARD," while the thing on the wall is a "BLACK-board," and that's no accident. The way we mark *blackboard* as "a thing," different from just any old board that happens to be black, is with the Backshift. A *blackboard* is something very specific—"a thing," as it were.

It's the same with a black bird, which is what we would call some probably uglyish bird of any number of strains, and a blackbird, the one variety taxonomized as *Turdus merula*. (*Turdus* just means thrush in Latin!) *Blackbird* is pronounced "BLACK-bird" because of the Backshift. The Backshift is in you: it is a rule of English that we all know without having to work at it. You know, for example, that Backshift itself is pronounced "BACK-shift," not "back-SHIFT," which would sound like someone trying to imitate William Powell. How did you know? Because I am discussing the Backshift as an established process, and to speak English is to know that when something is "a thing," it has the accent on the first syllable. If someone described what they called, say, a lethal shift, then spontaneously you would pronounce it as a "lethal SHIFT." That's because it's hard to even imagine what a lethal shift would be, it is most certainly not "a thing," and therefore no Backshift happens. Note how much more graceful *paradigm shift* sounds when we acccent the *paradigm* rather than the *shift*—"PARADIGM shift" is more likely than "paradigm SHIFT." That's because *paradigm shift* is an established concept.

What we're seeing is words coming together to become new ones. *Black* and *board* became parts of a new word, *blackboard*. Or, *ice* and *cream* became parts of a new word *ice cream*. *Ice cream* is two words? Well, that depends on what you consider a word to be, and writing conventions don't help us much in deciding. Writing, inherently conservative, changes with the language only in fits and starts. English's spelling system, as we have seen, blithely conserves the pronunciations of people very, very dead.

Therefore the fact that we write *ice cream* as two words can't be taken as an indication that it actually is, in some self-standing way, two words. In our minds, in our mouths, is it? When a toddler is learning about ice cream with the requisite enthusiasm, do we really think they feel themselves as saying *ice* and *cream* rather than something which in an alternate universe we would write as "icecream"? Ice cream is only abstractly icy, after all: unless it's been improperly stored, there are no tooth-rattling ice crystals in it; nor is it hard like, say, icicles or even Popsicles. Then, to the extent that we regularly encounter cream, if it has a consistency anything like ice cream it's in the form of hand or face cream, which we do not eat. To muse upon the fact that ice cream is supposed to be some kind of iced cream, or cream of ice, is actually very much a matter of musing, not intuition. It's a bit of a head-scratcher, and that's because *ice cream* is really a single thing of its own. It is, in a sense, one word, and a key indication of that is that it has submitted to the Backshift. ICE cream, not ice CREAM.

The Backshift in Real Life

The recruitment of words into serving as parts of new ones is one more way that a word is one stage in an endless transformation. Even if aware of how words have changed, however, we find it easy to suppose that this kind of change was tolerable in the past but somehow less appropriate in the present. The Backshift beautifully demonstrates the ineluctable timelessness of language change, however, in that we can see the Backshift operating on words in real time.

It can happen pretty quickly, and I write this in the wake of an entire century that was amply recorded. Moreover, much of that recording is today available at the press of a button. Thus while today blackboards, blackbirds, and ice cream have been around for what seems like forever, the Backshift got to many things much more recently, explaining what otherwise sounds as if people in the recent past simply talked strangely.

For example, in a *Mr. Magoo* cartoon in 1955 ("Magoo's Check-up"), a television pitchman advertises what he calls a "super-MARKET." But today we say "SUPER-market"— what was wrong with that voice-over artist? Or with William Holden when he says *supermarket* the same way in a voice-over in *Sunset Boulevard* (1950)? Nothing. The term was still newish in 1955, and when first coined, was intended as referring to a market that is super, as in bigger than the mom-and-pop stores that had been standard until then. One said, at first, a "downright super MARKET." But as supermarkets became the default way of buying food in

America, complete with particular associations such as parking lots, public address system announcements, that particular smell of the meat section, and express lines, the Backshift happened: hence SUPER-market. As late as 1964, a very obscure Broadway musical lyric was set to a melody line that accented *supermarket* on the MARKET, and I used to think of it as a small artistic slip in scansion. But then I learned about the Backshift, upon which I knew that the lyricist, born and raised before supermarkets were default, would have been familiar with the old pronunciation, such that it would have sounded appropriate to him when scanned to the melody in that way, even though he may not have regularly said "super-MARKET" himself.*

After that, it also made perfect sense to me that on episodes of *Dr. Kildare*, from around the same time, characters sometimes refer to what's on an "x-RAY" rather than an "X-ray." The Backshift hadn't set in completely on the word yet—people for whom the X-ray was a novel concept, as in "some ray that is the kind called X" in the vein of "some bird that is black," would say "x-RAY" for a while. "X-ray," with the Backshift, like *blackbird* and *ice cream*, would have come later. In a 1937 movie (*Ali Baba Goes to Town*) the grand old singing comic Eddie Cantor talks about serving people "hot DOGs" instead of HOT dogs, and he isn't referring to heating up Saint Bernards. It's just that the expression had been newer when he learned to talk in the 1890s, and thus less completely Backshifted. For the same reason, Cantor's very last line in *Strike Me Pink*, in 1936, is about what he calls the

---

* I know some people will ask, so: "Addy's at It Again," from *I Had a Ball*.

"boy SCOUTS." The Boy Scouts had begun just twenty-six years before; Backshift was still optional.

The "Why?" melts away, especially when we think more of what has become "a thing" than of what arbitrary formalities require us to write as two words. Phil Silvers as Sergeant Bilko in the late 1950s called the gum "Juicy FRUIT" instead of "JUICY Fruit" as we say it today. Why? Because it was newer then, so one could say Juicy Fruit the way you'd refer to actual fruit that was juicy. "What do want after lunch, Paul?" someone might ask. He wouldn't answer, "I'll have some nice JUICY fruit," unless he wanted to emphasize *juicy* because last night you gave him dried figs. Otherwise he'd ask for more of that "juicy FRUIT." To Silvers in the 1950s, however, the name of the gum still, to an extent, corresponded to what it referred to: juicy FRUIT. Or, in one of those snappy, naughty little pre–Production Code movies (*Skyscraper Souls*, 1932), someone disparages someone else for wanting to be a "big SHOT," not a "BIG shot." The expression was newer then—someone at the time was still referring, on some level, to an actual shot in the sense of a gunshot or cannon shot. Note that we today would rarely even think of big shot as referring to a shot. It has long been, really, one word *bigshot*—thus pronounced "BIG shot"—just as *gunshot* and *buckshot* are. We just don't write it that way.

You can even see the Backshift happening in living color. In an episode of *The Mary Tyler Moore Show* in the early 1970s, Mary Richards and some other characters order what they call Chinese FOOD. With the color photography and the fact that people in the early '70s considered themselves so resplendently modern, what with hippies, discotheques, and the Pill, it looks odd now to see these people saying Chinese FOOD rather than what we would say today: CHINESE food. The Backshift makes sense of it. In the early '70s, Chinese food wasn't mainstream yet; it was still an exotic novelty. Therefore, one would not yet have pronounced it with the Backshift. I'd bet a lot of money that about ten years after that episode was taped, Mary Tyler Moore and Valerie Harper (playing Rhoda), now as accustomed to Chinese food as the rest of America became, started saying CHINESE food.

You don't even need to listen to the past: the Backshift tells you what you would have heard anyway. With *French fry*—again, it's two words more on paper than in reality—in our minds, are we really thinking about Frenchness at all when we say it? When the Republicans tried to get us to call them Freedom fries during their irritation with the French in the run-up to the Iraq War in 2003, much of the reason it was so funny was that French fries are not French in our minds in any real way. French fries are "a thing" in themselves, quite apart from any literal conception of a "fry" (whatever *that* exactly is) prepared in a French way. However, certainly, at a point they were still processed as fries that are French—people didn't start calling them that for no reason. Therefore, we can know that "FRENCH fry" must be a Backshift pronunciation of something that started as "French FRY." And it was indeed: as late as 1966, the *Random House Unabridged Dictionary* was giving the "French FRY" pronunciation, and recently I have heard octogenarians say "French FRY" rather than "FRENCH fry." People of that age at this writing have witnessed the Backshift making *French* and *fry* into a new word: "Frenchfry."

One last one: on an episode of *The Dick Van Dyke Show* the same year Lucy was buying her maid the broasted chicken, a woman of a certain age refers to a "crossword PUZZLE." Odd way to say it—until we realize that the actress, Arlene Harris, was born in 1896 and crossword puzzles became popular only in the 1920s. That's the way it would have been said when she learned the word as a young woman, and she stuck with it. To be *Boardwalk Empire/Mad Men*–style obsessively accurate about getting the past right, people saying *crossword puzzle* in a play or movie set in the 1920s or '30s should pronounce it "crossword PUZZLE," and older people depicted in the 1950s and '60s should say it that way, too. Because, well, some people (me) will notice.

As with anything in language, the Backshift exhibits some irregularities. It's hard to say, for example, why *street* forces the Backshift while *avenue* doesn't: BROAD Street, WASHINGTON Street, but Fifth AVENUE, Kennedy AVENUE. It isn't that *avenue* is a longer word, because if that were the solution, then why Penny LANE, Allens LANE?* These are

---

* *Allens Lane* may seem oddly specific, and it is: it's a street in Philadelphia in my childhood neighborhood, occupied by a camp as it has been since I was a kid and before. The camp did a (nonmusical) production of *Cinderella* in the early '70s, and despite the low-tech facilities, I recall as clear as day that the Fairy Godmother actually did change Cinderella's dress into a different one with a wave of her wand. I am 95 percent sure this isn't a distorted childhood memory. What I recall is a very real live female person standing there onstage, suddenly granted a different dress in a flash. For forty-plus years I have been wondering how they did that.

things that intrigue the professionals. More generally, however, the sheer tendency fascinates nevertheless: grammar below the radar that creates new words out of old ones. For example, you now are in a position to know why old-timers pronounced Broadway "broad-WAY."

Lexical Mitosis: When Words Reproduce

Products of the Backshift are "new words" to varying degrees. We can't help perceiving the two elements *black* and *board* surviving within the word *blackboard,* even if their meanings are now abstractified. Most readily, we perceive *blackboard* as "two words in one," but still, two of something. Linguists even call these kinds of words *compounds,* with its acknowledgment that even as "one word," the product is something less than totally unitary. But things, as so often, go farther. Words that date can go on to mate.

First can come what we could think of as the commitment. Because it involves only one of the words, it may seem more like codependency, but we're all adults here. Often if a word is part of the unaccented part of the compound, then it starts being pronounced more fuzzily, and drifts ever farther beyond what we would think of as a word in any sense at all.

Take *policeman, fireman, clergyman, postman,* and *gentleman*: one does not pronounce the *-man* part the way one would pronounce *man* by itself. Rather, you say something like "mun," a sludgy "whatever" kind of pronunciation. That has happened over the years, as the words have undergone what you could call enunciational wear. Originally, the -*man* in these words was pronounced fully, but now, if someone had no idea how English was written and heard words like *policeman* and *fireman*, they might not even associate the little -*mun* with the word *man* at all.

One way we know that this pronunciation of -*man* develops gradually over time is that if you start all over again and make up a new word with -*man* on the end, you will usually pronounce the -*man* fully. *Anchorman* and *caveman* are newish concepts; yes, cavemen themselves date pretty far back, but what taught us that they existed was paleontology, which does not. Therefore those two words are pronounced with "man" rather than "mun."

After that, chance plays its role as always: sometimes fate spares a -*man*. *Postman* is pronounced "post-mun," but there's no such thing as a "mail-mun." However, the general tendency is what matters, as it explains, for example, why British people say "saucepun" for *saucepan*—it's because the Backshift left the -*pan* hanging, exposed to the elements. "Saucepun" sounds bracingly weird to the American ear, and yet it's no different from *forehead* when pronounced "FORE-id," as it commonly is. One no longer knows *head* was ever even part of the equation without the spelling, which reflects the stage when *fore* and *head* first came together at all, when *head* was still its own person instead of losing itself trying to live through *fore*.

But after a while, even the other word's pronunciation gets muddied up, and that's when dating finally gets to actual mating. *Cupboard* is a fine example. Only as written is *cupboard* in any sense two words; *cup* is as lost in the shuffle as *board*. Learning it as a child, one hears simply a single word "cubberd," and has no idea that the word refers to a board you put cups on, which, today, it does not anyway. *Breakfast* is similar: we think not of breaking a fast but of "breckfist," a single word for a certain meal taken early in the day. That "break" and "fast" were originally the word's parts qualifies as a fun fact, available only upon learning the conservative spelling of the word. This is also the reason for those odd nautical pronunciations such as "bowson" for *boatswain* and "fokesul" for *forecastle*. Then even if one word's pronunciation is still intact, that word's meaning may give so little clue to what the pairing means that we've essentially hit *cupboard* territory anyway. When *main sail* became "main-sul," the "-sul" left no clue that the reference was a sail, but just about anything can be "main." In the same way, to link the *fore-* in *forehead* with frontness is a bit of a stretch: it's on the "fore" of your head, but more immediately we think of it as above the eyes. Besides, in regions such as where I grew up, where the word is pronounced "FAHR-id" rather than "FORE-id," the connection really was completely lost anyway.

This is also how *daisy* originated from *day's eye*: say *day's eye* fast enough and note that you are, one, bored and, two, saying *daisy*. That describes how that word emerged in the mouths of English speakers over time, but the difference with *breakfast* is that with *daisy*, even the spelling gives nothing away. There is sex in the history of quite a few words that seem quite untouched. *World* is one. In *werewolf*, the *were-* part once meant "man," which is why *were*wolves are half man and half wolf. *World* began as *wer-eld*, where *wer* was that "man" word and *eld* meant "old," as in age. *Wer-eld* meant "man's age," as in "the age of man," as in man's time on earth. Gradually, via implication, it came to mean the earth itself: hence, today's *world*. *Bring* started as two words in Proto-Indo-European, the one we now have as "to bear," as in carry, and another one, *enk*, meaning "to get to" (*enk* later became *enough*). People were saying "to carry something and get it to a place," which is what bringing is. *Bherenk*, said a whole lot over thousands of years, becomes *bring*. Or *bridal* only looks like *bride* with the *-al* on the end that we recognize from *final* and *total*. The word started as a reference to a feast connected with a wedding: the *bride-ale*. The word *about* is not the scion of some ancient Old English word like "ægboþe," but a melding of *at*, *by*, and *out*.*

Backing Up, Dropping Off:
On the Street and in Your Life

A final way the Backshift makes new words is when the second word gets tired and drops off, leaving just the first one in a brand-new meaning. For example, again, in old movies and television shows, you can hear people referring to pizza as "pizza pie," pronounced "PIZZA pie." So, *pizza*

---

* For a sense of how words coming together is a key process in making a language what it is, there is a laudably readable, compact article by Paul Hopper that helped form my perspectives long ago, "Where Do Words Come From?," *Studies in Typology and Diachrony*, ed. by William Croft, Keith Denning, and Suzanne Kemmer (Amsterdam: John Benjamins, 1990), pp. 151–60.

started as short for *pizza pie*. This you can catch happening in 1956 on an episode of *The Honeymooners* when Alice refers once to pizza pie and then later to just pizza. But that cannot have been the whole story of *pizza*. If originally the idea was that pizza was a kind of tomato and cheese tart, which it is, then based on *blackboard* and *French fry* and the rest, we can know that at first, people must have thought of it as a *pizza kind of pie* as opposed to another kind, in which case they must have said "pizza PIE," before the Backshift happened.

And before YouTube happened, I would have had to be satisfied with asking bewildered elderly people about this, who likely have gotten so much in the habit of saying just pizza that they wouldn't remember whether they once said "pizza PIE" (and wouldn't care). But now I know that there are ancient 1950s TV commercials hawking, for example, what must have been a repulsive substance designed to allow Mrs. America to delight her bairns by bringing home "pizza PIE" in a can!

Therefore, one, pizza PIE, two, PIZZA pie, and three, pizza, a word Americans before World War II would have heard as some random "Eye-talian" word. (Franklin D. Roosevelt may never have tasted pizza.) In my own life, I have experienced "cellular PHONE"—a prop in a play I was involved with in 1993 when certain characters were sporting "cellular PHONES" as an indication of their obsession with money—becoming "CELL phone." Remember, circa 2000, "I only use my 'CELL phone' for emergencies," said by people already actually spending half their lives on their CELL phones? Or at least so much of their lives that rapidly the term became just "cell"? Talking on a cell, to someone as late as 1990, would have sounded as incoherent as something a Timothy Leary would have come up with in his more, well, enlightened moments. *Cell* in reference to a phone happened because of the Backshift, followed by what we could call the Dropoff.

Words you'd never suspect have the Dropoff in their past. *Road* in Old English meant a ride, not a path. When in Shakespeare's *Henry VIII*, Griffith recounts to Katherine the demise of Cardinal Wolsey, he mentions that after being so sick that the cardinal could no longer ride his mule, later "with easy roads, he came to Leicester." Today it sounds like Shakespeare was referring to smooth carriage trails, but Shakespeare may well have been referring to easy rides, as in gentler horses. *Roadway*, as in "riding path," was the term that meant what we mean by *road* today. After a while, though, people started dropping the *-way* off and saying just *road* for short, now to refer to a path instead of a ride.

Words are on the move, then, right here in life as we are living it. I once heard someone on the street talking (on his CELL) about the "re-PEAT stress" plaguing him. It took me a bit to process what this utterance that sounded like "PEES-treh" was. It sounded like it was perhaps another kind of Italian pastry. But no—he meant what not too long ago all people were pronouncing as the novel term "repeat STRESS syndrome." The Backshift on the streets, backing up, dropping off—it's everywhere. Listen for living language!

When Words Mate on the Sly

The analogy between languages and animal reproduction can go only so far. For example, languages do not evolve according to fitness the way creatures do. Of course they retain words for what they need words for, but French's subjunctive and German's three genders are not adaptive. They are accidental overgrowth that languages accrete as inevitably as words change their meanings.

Yet the analogy can get us quite far. For example, we have learned that *Homo sapiens* of European heritage carry DNA sequences from Neanderthals, as a result of matings long ago. In the same way, words can leave chunks of themselves inside other words, replacing the original material with a new one. The word lives on, and no one bats an eye.

Or sometimes they do, especially lately in the case of common sentiments about how some people pronounce *nuclear* as "nucular." Commonly treated as a mere matter of messiness, "nucular" is actually another example of word sex.

Typically we hear of "nucular" that it's an ignorant mistake because the word is *nuclear* in the dictionary. However, I hope that this book has gotten across the point that the dictionary has no sacrosanct authority in telling us how a word "is" pronounced in some cosmically unquestionable way. Rather, the dictionary tells us how a word happens to be pronounced, often by most but not all people, at the time it is compiled.

Now, if only one person said "nucular"—an impression some seem to have had of George W. Bush, whose use of the "nucular" pronunciation seemed to give complaints about it a new urgency—then it would qualify as an eccentricity, and therefore as a mistake. "If the way so many people talk is okay, then what counts as a mistake?" a linguist is often asked. The answer is: when people are doing things on their own. I once knew someone who, for some reason, despite otherwise perfectly ordinary American English, used "ner-fry" for *nursery* and "grofery" for *grocery*. That was, quite simply, off because no one else says the words that way; nor is there anything about their sounds that makes it likely that anyone ever will.

But in fact, a great many people say "nucular," including educated people. In a case like that, we might seek to know why so many people pronounce it that way, and more to the point, we might seek a reason more systematic than that people simply "screw it up." There exists such a systematic reason. People say "nucular" modeled on other words that end in *-ular* such as *spectacular, tubular,* and *vernacular*. Specifically, because there exist the words *nuke* and, long before that, *nucleus,* a temptation looms to think of *nuclear* as "nuc-" plus the *-ular* ending: *spectacular, tubular, nuc-ular*. This means that the *-ular* ending on so many words made its way into *nuclear,* infecting and remodeling it just as snippets of Neanderthal DNA did to European *Homo sapiens*.

This may sound like special pleading for a word that we can't help hearing as a tad ignorant-sounding if we haven't adopted it ourselves. However, the process is actually normal in how a language changes. There are only so many sounds, and although the ways they can combine creates a vast variety of words, there will be times when a sequence of sounds in a word we pronounce happens to resemble a sequence of sounds in another one.

A favorite of mine, although it will never catch on, is my older daughter's first pronunciation of *bathing suit* as "bathing soup"—she learned about soup first, and the *t* in *suit* doesn't sound unlike the *p* in *soup*—she also called suitcases "soupcases." Note, though, that you can almost imagine "soupcase" catching on, out of an idea of someone toting lots of cans of soup along on their trip, given that we tend to avoid actually carrying whole suits in suitcases and would more lucidly call them clothescases.* Things like "bathing soup" and "soupcase" do catch on when the "wrong" pronunciation ends up sounding even more logically plausible than cases for our soup on the road. Hence "nuc-ular," or examples that, now older, don't even sound like mistakes anymore.

For example, by all rights, the word *burger* is a mistake. The word had no ancestor in Old English or even Middle English. The word *burgher* traces that far back, indeed, but it refers to a certain kind of middle-class citizen, and clearly has nothing to do with Whoppers and Quarter Pounders. The *burger* so familiar to us was an accident.

It started with the fact that what we know as hamburger was initially called *Hamburg steak,* and a patty of it between bread called a *hamburger sandwich,* as opposed to the thing

---

* Sammy Davis Jr., late in his life, actually did travel with a full array of Campbell's soups when he toured. (Thank you to Terry Kelleher for the recollection.)

then known as *frankfurter sandwiches,* now called hot dogs.*
The relevant word was *Hamburg,* as in the German city. To
someone in the nineteenth century familiar with these
then-new terms, hearing what they were eating called a
"burger" would have sounded as odd as hearing somebody
call a burrito a "rito" now.

Except that *hamburger* lent a particular reason to start
saying *burger* eventually: the *ham* part. Ham is meat, and if
one didn't pause to think—and people had little more time
to indulge in that pastime then than they do now—it may
reasonably have sounded as if *hamburger sandwich* referred
to something made of ham. If so, it followed from what was
left of *hamburger* minus the *ham-* part was called a "burger."
The word *ham,* then, infected *hamburger sandwich,* in which
until then the *ham-* part of the word had been a random
sequence of syllables, the first sounds in the word *Hamburg.*

Hence, the notion of the "cheese burger" by the late
1930s, with "burger" now referring to a disk of meat. Today,
of course, one speaks of the veggie burger, taco burger, fish
burger, and so much else, such that no one would object
that burger is "not a word." Now it is, but only because of
grafting. We talk about eating a nice burger, and Abraham
Lincoln brought back to life would picture us trying to
consume a staid, small-town German tradesman.

---

* One has not lived, frankly, until one has seen a certain Harry Rose perform an old song called "Frankfurter Sandwiches" in an early talkie
short in 1929. Due to the miracles of modern technology, one can now see
it at the press of a button on YouTube. I won't even describe this marvelous two minutes; just take a look. It has delighted legions of guests in my
house.

Or what's a seacopter? Or a medicopter? You can imagine, because you know what a copter is. But technically you shouldn't. The idea of *copter* as short for *helicopter* chops the word in a place its coiners would have found unnatural. *Helico* means spiral and *pter* "wing." Both roots are Greek and, by themselves, fairly recognizable; we all know what a helix is, and *pter* also made it into *pterodactyl*. However, in English we don't spontaneously process *pt* as the beginning of a word or even a syllable, and so *helico-pter* most readily comes out as "heli-copter." Then the DNA/"soupcase" business comes in. The *-er* in *-copter* seems like the same one in *blender, flyer,* and *tiller,* rather than just the tail end of a weird syllable *pter*. That makes it easy to shorten *helicopter* into "copter," as in "that which copts." But what's "copting"? Well, we might figure *copt* was perhaps the Greek root lost to us, when actually if *copt* were the root, then the ancient creatures would be called *coptodactyls*—which would be kind of neat, but only because of our initially mistaken sense of how *helicopter* parses out!

This kind of mishearing has given us a goofy prefix and a goofy suffix as well. To anyone before the late nineteenth century, *chocoholic, textaholic,* and certainly *sexaholic* would have sounded as odd as *A Clockwork Orange*'s Nadsat. "What in blazes," they would harrumph, "is 'holic'? Where do you get such balderdash?" We get it from *alcoholic*, which even to us, upon reflection, divides as *alcohol+ic*. However, folk impression developed a sense that the part signaling addiction was *-holic* rather than just *-ic*. A "-holic" strand of DNA broke off, born of a suffix trailing a goodly stub of what was once the word behind it, like a drumstick that comes off with the thigh attached. This new hunk of material, rather than just -*ic* by itself, was processed as meaning "addict." This -*holic* started attaching to other words, and here we are. Our modern -*holic* words may seem mere jokes, but claims that a suffix now so entrenched and fertile is "not real" lead to a question as to just how we define reality. *Workaholic*, in particular, is hardly slang or a passing witticism.

Then, *cybervision, cyberoptics, cybermarketing, cyberculture*—all these words are flubs, technically. It started with *cybernetics*, from the Greek word *kybernetes*, for "steersman." *Cybernetics* was composed, then, of *cybern* (not *cyber*) plus -*etics*. But most of us don't know Greek, and *cyber*- seemed the more intuitive first element than *cybern*.

Hence cyberattacks instead of cybernattacks, just as here and there in Europeans' DNA there are those stutters of Neanderthal. You can't get them out of there, and so we might as well say, *Vive la différence!* After all, the people who actually say, *Vive la différence* have Neanderthal genes in them, and last time I checked, they were associated with at least some degree of sophistication.

Here We Go Again

When words come together, the new word is subject to the very processes of change we have seen in previous chapters. The familiarity that signals the Backshift is pragmatic, or personal, in the sense discussed in chapter 1. There is a web of sentiments around *big shot*, mostly suspicious. Such feelings are more subjective than the ones a term like *influential person* inspires. *Gentleman* began in the meaning of "a man who is genteel," as in of noble birth. That is hardly what we mean in saying "The gentleman over there needs your help," in which case referring to the man as a gentleman has become a courtesy that means, basically, "not a slob." That's an example of how implication changes words' meanings over time, as we saw in chapter 2. The muffled way *man* is pronounced in words like *gentleman* and *fireman* suggests that it is becoming more of a suffix than a word. In other words, that *man* is grammaticalizing à la chapter 3. *Man* is "trying" to become the equivalent of the suffix *-er*, as in *hunter*. This actually happened with the product name *Walkman*, where the item was distinctly ungendered and thus Walkman meant "the thing you walk with," just as *walker* can mean "the thing that an elderly person might walk with." Finally, when that new word hits the ground, sound change starts messing around with it, as we saw with *cupboard, breakfast, daisy,* and *forehead,* so that after a while you may not even be able to tell the word used to be a pair.

This churn is eternal in a language, always helping replenish the language's word stock. *Barn* started as "barley-arn" for barley house; *arn* is now a lost word, but a dormitory was once a "sleep-arn," a guesthouse was a "guest-arn," and so on. But now we'd never know *barn*, such a gruff old stump of a word, was ever more than one of anything, and today it is part of the Backshifted *barnyard*. Then, say *barnyard humor*—do you say "BARNYARD humor" rather than "barnyard HUMOR"? If so, there's a new Backshift, due to the popularity of this brand of wit.

Compounding, then, is central to how a language comes to be what it is. It is easy to miss how common it is in English: writing conventions often hide it (*ice cream*), and the Backshift is something subconscious that requires pointing out. However, a book like this written for Germans would not have to call its speakers' attention to compounding, as that language is fond of highway pileups like *Wohnwagenparkplatzeinwohnerklagen* (mobile home parking lot residents' complaints). Chinese consists of about four hundred single short syllables (*li, wu, ma, lan,* etc.), which have four tones that they can occur on. That yields just sixteen hundred possible words,* nowhere near enough to furnish a language's vocabulary, which requires tens of thousands of words at the very least. Homonymy (e.g., *bat* as an animal and *bat* as a sporting implement) can be handy, especially with the support of context. But a language in which each syllable with a tone had dozens of meanings would not be processible by human brains. For this reason, in Chinese most words have to be compounds, with the endless possible combinations of the syllables allowing the language the massive vocabulary it needs. Rendered in Chinese, the first sentence of the Declaration of Independence is practically all compounds, for example. In the phrase "When in the course of human events," *human* is "have-concern man-type," *events* is "matter-affair," and *course* is "send-unfold proceed-order."

---

* Fewer, actually, because not all the possible syllable-tone combinations exist; there are holes in the "grid."

In English, compounding is less dramatic but still central to the way we end up expressing ourselves. It is one more way that language does not just sit, formed. It moves, forming. What seems almost designed to keep us from delighting in, or even perceiving, this endless show is the printed page. Please read a few more of them, nevertheless, in the final chapter, where I will explain.

6

This Is Your Brain on Writing

Lingering Questions

I am espousing a view of language as eternally mutable, and yet it still may not seem quite plausible. Language change may seem like scurvy or being eaten by a bear: something the ancients had to put up with that we are more or less past.

The main thing that encourages that perspective is that our most spontaneous conception of language, always and forever, will be writing. Writing is what it seems language actually is. And writing doesn't seem terribly mutable.

We think of ourselves as speaking writing, rather than as writing speech, even though writing has existed for only 6,500 years, whereas speech likely traces back to the dawn of our species 150,000 years ago. One talks less of the sounds in one's language than of the letters in it. A speech variety rarely written is dismissed as a mere "dialect," with status as a real language indicated by writing, even though all but about two hundred languages out of six thousand are barely written at all.

This is your brain on writing: If someone says "dog," you might picture a dog, but if someone says "already," you picture the word as written. But imagine if you could neither read nor write and someone said "already." You would likely imagine some scenario in which that word played a part, possibly one early in your life, when you were learning how to use the word. Yet with our brains on writing, we imagine the word as scratched out in arbitrarily agreed-upon symbols—and in the case of English speakers, symbols ensnared into a senseless system besides. Why does *ea* stand for "eh" in *bread* but for "ee" in *meat*? Why does *y* stand for "ee" in *early* but not in *yak*? It's a crazy thing in its way, this business of thinking of language as writing. But we're stuck with it.

And one thing about writing is that it stays put. It just sits there. Its stationary quality implies constancy, tradition—law. This is much of why the English spelling system remains in place despite its absurdity: it's cast in stone. The folk song mutates endlessly over time as the melody and words change from mouth to mouth, generation over generation. Mozart's Symphony No. 40 will always be played the same way, however, because it's written. The writing of language exerts a similar kind of influence. It suggests that things aren't supposed to change.

Moreover, this very air of judgment that writing casts over speech actually does make language change more slowly than it otherwise would, as long as writing permeates society and literacy is widespread enough that a critical mass of people can read. Shakespeare in 1600 could not have functioned at all in the Old English of six hundred years before, whereas he could get around pretty well now, four hundred years later. Much of this is because education and literacy increased by leaps and bounds after his time, such that the typical Anglophone brain was a brain on writing. By the eighteenth century, it was standard to feel that one was supposed to speak not simply in the way that felt natural, but in a certain way that was enshrined on paper. The page held the language back from rolling along as heartily as it had in earlier times.

However, to understand that language is inherently mutable regardless of sociohistorical conditions, we need a revised sense of the trajectory from *Beowulf* to *Breaking Bad*. If you find it hard to truly believe that it's normal for a language to change as much as English did from Old English to *King Lear* in just six hundred years, you're onto something. Language does not normally transform so vastly in such a brief period. But then, even in the mouths of those of us whose brains are on writing, over on the other side of the Shakespearean divide, English has changed a lot more since Shakespeare than we think. In the grand scheme of things, change treads along at a moderate pace, but unstoppable.

For example, the transformation of English between *Beowulf* and Shakespeare was indeed especially disruptive, not business as usual. The Old English of *Beowulf* was vastly retooled in terms of grammar when it was imposed on the Celtic people who inhabited Britain before the first English speakers arrived. Then the Vikings drastically simplified the grammar, turning a language like German into the much less grammatically cluttered English we know and love (like?). Finally, English was then drenched in a fire hose spray of new words from French and later Latin. All three of these things together made Middle English much more unlike Old English than, for example, modern German is different from Old High German. Short of some unprecedented historical upheavals, the English of the year 2500 will be in no way as different from today's English as Shakespeare's was from Old English.

But then, we are farther from the English of 1600 than we know. Nothing makes this clearer than the fact, mentioned in chapter 2, of how easy it is to attend a Shakespearean play and find much of the language opaque when delivered live. Some may hold to the idea that this isn't the case when the actors are British and especially well trained, but those who would disagree may be familiar with the experience of attending a perfectly fine rendition of *Macbeth* and finding it all but impossible to draw sense out of most of the words going by without previous study. The simple reason is that English has changed more vastly since 1600 than it may seem. We will recall *Lear*'s Edmund complaining about the "curiosity of nations" and describing himself as "generous," using meanings unrecoverable today when heard live without prior instruction. Despite the reactionary tendency that writing exerts, English has gone on changing.

Shakespeare seems so very long ago, though, such that it may seem that maybe English was different *waaaay* back then, but that things have pretty much settled into a certain permanent place since, perhaps, about two hundred years ago, other than new names for new things. In fact, not. The first clue that more is changing even now than we suppose is things we have already seen: bobbling accents on words and the Backshifts clicking into place here, there, and everywhere all the time. But there's more. For example, instead of going back to the seventeenth century, what about just the nineteenth? The English of *Moby-Dick* is interesting in that Herman Melville was writing in a language more removed from ours than we would expect of a book that was only a hundred-and-a-bit years old during the Eisenhower administration. In fact, much of why the book is a majestic and yet often taxing read is not only the almost obsessive detail about whaling and the mile-long sentences, but also that Melville often means something different with a word from what we're used to. It can make his writing feel like a radio station not quite tuned in right.

For example, early on, Ishmael mentions that something is "more wonderful than that an iceberg should be moored to one of the Moluccas." But would seeing an iceberg tied to a tropical island make us exclaim, "Great that that's finally happened! What will they think of next!" Would we find it "wonderful"? Elsewhere, Ishmael mentions the "wonderfulness and fearfulness of the rumors"—but does he really mean to describe rumors as being neato and scary at the same time? That's a little idiosyncratic, no? After a while one understands that by *wonderful*, Melville was referring to actual wonder, something that occasions marveling, usually in the vein of finding something strange, not "cool." Of Ahab, second mate Stubb says, "Oh! he's a wonderful old man!"

But even those who haven't savored the book likely know that Ahab is hardly someone typically called "wonderful"— he is a broken, humorless obsessive, "wonderful" only in the sense of, say, an iceberg washing up in Bermuda. The word's meaning has changed since 1851. Today Stubb would say that Ahab was curious or peculiar, just as Charles Darwin would likely call the flesh-eating Venus flytrap plant bizarre rather than wonderful, as he did in 1892.

Pitiful throws one in Moby-Dick, too. "The port is pitiful," we learn, expecting a couple of lean-tos and a dying pelican. But no, "in the port is safety, comfort, hearthstone, supper, warm blankets, friends, all that's kind to our mortalities." By pitiful, Melville meant "showing or feeling pity," again clear in his other usages. On the ocean, "a black cloud, rising up with earnest of squalls and rains"—"with earnest"? What is the place of sincerity in a rain cloud? The best we may do here is suppose that "with earnest" meant "vigorously"; more likely we just read on. But earnest could mean "promise" in earlier English, and Melville's English was earlier than ours. Earlier as in his description of sharks "hilariously" swarming about a whale corpse, where he was using the word to mean "high-spirited," from which our sense of "very amusing" is understandable but not the one that occurred readily to him in his time. We today have the fading expression willy-nilly and learn that it came from the old form nill for "I will not," but Meville could still write the actual words: "Will I nill I, the ineffable thing has tied me to him." He can still use bridal by itself as a noun— originally the bride-ale as in party. For him, facsimile is still a fac simile, as in Latin for "make similar." And Melville was quite fond of the word *whelm*, whereas we long ago gave that up for *overwhelm*.

In *Moby-Dick*, these signs of change come roughly once every couple of pages. Two hundred fifty years earlier, in Shakespeare's plays such signs of change are much more common, and are more of a barrier to comprehension because change has proceeded for a longer time. Two centuries before that is Chaucerian English, which truly requires translation to connect with.

And then here, on the other end, in the 1880s Doctor Sloper in Henry James's novel *Washington Square* describes his sister, Aunt Penniman, as *fantastic* and *artificial*. However, neither word makes sense if we read them in their modern meaning. Doctor Sloper doesn't think much of his sister, and therefore is not giving her a compliment in calling her fantastic—he means that she is given to embracing romantic fantasies and poking into people's business with them. The meaning is preserved for us in the meaning of *fantastical*, but in James's day, *fantastic*, too, still had the meaning, which we can see was once thought of as the "real" one, in terms of what a fantasy actually is. No one in 1880 would have named a cleaning fluid Fantastik. Then, *artificial*, applied to Aunt Penniman, has a similar meaning: she likes to fashion social life into dramatic concoctions; today we would call her a drama queen. Note the chance aspect of these things: *fantastic* has since become a compliment, while *artificial* is now a put-down when, as we saw, it once could mean "pleasingly elaborate."

Then, as recently as a century ago, F. Scott Fitzgerald has Nick Buchanan in *The Great Gatsby* say, "It's been proved," where most of us today would find *proved* a little off, having expected *proven*. But *proved* wasn't an attempt by Fitzgerald to give a hint of Buchanan's limited intellect. *Proved* was a perfectly ordinary past participle form for *prove* in the 1920s; James uses it in *Washington Square*, too, for example. *Proven* became the default only after the 1960s. People in the *Gatsby* period would also have been comfortable with *dived* and *sneaked* instead of *dove* and *snuck*. Past and participial forms are always churning. Take, if I may, *shat* as the past of *shit*: one often feels it as a tad poetic or arch, but then note that *shitted* sounds awkward somehow, while to just say, *He shit two mornings ago*, doesn't really work, either. Or does it?

These things are ever in flux; the changing is all there is. In our mouths or in print, in villages or in cities, in buildings or in caves, a language doesn't sit still. It can't. Language change has proceeded apace even in places known for preserving a language in amber. Modern Arabic speakers can speak and understand the ancient language of the Qur'an, but this is due to a deliberate retention of that language in its original state for purposes of religion and formal communication. This required contravening something natural, and could work only for a variety enshrined by writing and strict oral memorization practices. Arabic as it has come down to modern times in spoken form is, in each location, a different language from the standard, with the local standards all different from one another. The Moroccan who speaks "Arabic" actually speaks both the standard and the Moroccan descendant of it, which are so different that it is equivalent to someone who speaks Latin and Spanish. Or you may have heard that Icelanders can still read the ancient sagas written almost a thousand years ago in Old Norse. It is true that *written* Icelandic is quite similar to Old Norse, but the spoken language is quite different—first, in vocabulary, as we would expect, both in terms of new words and the evolution of meanings; then also, the modern language's vowels have drifted quite a bit, just as we would also expect. Old Norse speakers would sound a tad extraterrestrial to modern Icelanders. There have also been assorted changes in the grammar—nothing as radical as what makes Modern English different from Old, but language has moved on, on that distant isle as everywhere else.

Like, Wow!: Is *Any* New Thing Really Just Business as Usual?

Under this view of language, as something becoming rather than being, a film rather than a photo, in motion rather than at rest, we are now prepared to address a topic that many may have considered an odd omission in the book so far: the way young people use (drum roll, please) *like*. So deeply reviled, so hard on the ears of so many, so new, and with such an air of the unfinished, of insecurity and even dimness, the new *like* is hard to, well, love. However, it takes on a different aspect when we see that it is a splendid demonstration of everything we have seen in this book.

First, let's take *like* in just its traditional, accepted forms. Even in its dictionary definition, *like* is the product of stark changes in meaning that no one would ever guess. To an

Old English speaker, the word that later became *like* was the word for, of all things, "body"! The word was *lic*, and *lic* was part of a word, *gelic*, that meant "with the body," as in "with the body of," which was a way of saying "similar to"—as in *like*. *Gelic* over time shortened to just *lic*, which became *like*. Of course, there were no days when these changes happened abruptly and became official. It was just that, step by step, the syllable *lic*, which to an Old English speaker meant "body," came to mean, when uttered by people centuries later, "similar to"—and life went on.

Like has become a piece of grammar: it is the source of the suffix *-ly*. To the extent that *slowly* means "in a slow fashion," as in "with the quality of slowness," it is easy (and correct) to imagine that *slowly* began as "slow-like," with *like* gradually wearing away into a *-ly* suffix. That historical process is especially clear in that there are still people who, colloquially, say *slow-like, angry-like*. Technically, *like* yielded two suffixes, because *-ly* is also used with adjectives, as in *portly* and *saintly*. Again, the pathway from *saint-like* to *saintly* is not hard to perceive.

Like doesn't sound the way it once did. In Old English, *lic* was pronounced "leek." In our vowel chart, it occupied the *beet* slot. But we saw what happened to words in that slot in the Great Vowel Shift: *ee*s spewed off into being *igh*s. A word pronounced "leek" became *like*, just as a word pronounced "beet" became *bite*.

Like has become a part of compounds. *Likewise* began as *like* plus a word, *wise*, which was different from the one meaning "smart when either a child or getting old." This other *wise* meant "manner": *likewise* meant "similar in manner." This *wise* disappeared as a word on its own, and so now we think of it as a suffix, as in *clockwise* and *stepwise*. But we still have *likeminded*, where we can easily perceive *minded* as having independent meaning. Dictionaries tell us it's pronounced "like-MINE-did," but I, for one, say "LIKE-minded" and have heard many others do so—the Backshift Strikes Again!

Therefore, *like* is ever so much more than some isolated thing clinically described in a dictionary with a definition like "(*preposition*) 'having the same characteristics or qualities as; similar to.'" Think of a cold, limp, slimy squid splayed wet on a cutting board, its lifeless tentacles dribbling in coils, about to be sliced into calamari rings—in comparison to the brutally fleet, remorseless, dynamic creatures squid are when alive underwater—*like* as "(*preposition*) . . ." is wet on a cutting board.

There is a lot more to it: it swims, as it were. What we are seeing in *like*'s transformations today are just the latest chapters in a story that began with an ancient word that was supposed to mean "body." What we have seen in this book reveals the new *like* as just another day in the life of a word.

Like is a FACE marker. Because we think of *like* as meaning "akin to" or "similar to," kids decorating every sentence or two with it seems like overuse. After all, how often should a coherently minded person need to note that something is similar to something rather than just being that something? The new *like*, then, is associated with hesitation. It is common to label the newer generations as harboring a fear of venturing a definite statement.

That analysis seems especially appropriate in that this

usage of like *first* reached the national consciousness with its usage by Beatniks in the 1950s, as in "Like, wow!" We associate the Beatniks, as a prelude to the counterculture with their free-ranging aesthetic and recreational sensibilities, with relativism. Part of the essence of the Beatnik was a reluctance to be judgmental of anyone but those who would dare to (1) be judgmental themselves or (2) openly abuse others. However, the Beatniks were also associated with a certain griminess—why would others imitate *them*?—upon which it bears mentioning that the genealogy of the modern *like* traces farther back. Ordinary people, too, have long been using *like* as an appendage to indicate similarity with a trace of hesitation. The "slow-like" kind of usage is a continuation of this, and Saul Bellow has thoroughly un-Beatnik characters in his novels of the 1950s use *like* in a way we would expect a decade or two later. "That's the right clue and may do me some good. Something very big. Truth, like," says Tommy Wilhelm in *Seize the Day* (1956), a character raised in the 1910s and '20s, long before anyone had ever heard of a Beatnik. Bellow also has Henderson in *Henderson the Rain King* use *like* this way. Both Wilhelm and Henderson are tortured, galumphing characters riddled with uncertainty, but hippies they are not.

So today's *like* did not spring mysteriously from a crowd on the margins of unusual mind-set and then somehow jump the rails from them into the general population. The seeds of the modern *like* lay among ordinary people; the Beatniks may not even have played a significant role in what happened later. The point is that *like* transformed from something occasional into something more regular. Fade out, fade in: recently I heard a lad of roughly sixteen chatting with a friend about something that had happened the weekend before, and his utterance was—this is as close to verbatim as I can get: *So we got there and we thought we were going to have the room to ourselves and it turned out that like a family had booked it already. So we're standing there and there were like grandparents and like grandkids and aunts and uncles all over the place.* Anyone who has listened to American English over the past several decades will agree that this is thoroughly typical *like* usage.

The problem with the hesitation analysis is that this was a thoroughly confident speaker. He told this story with zest, vividness, and joy. What, after all, would occasion hesitation in spelling out that a family was holding an event in a room? It's real-life usage of this kind—to linguists it is data, just like climate patterns are to meteorologists—that suggests that the idea of *like* as the linguistic equivalent to slumped shoulders is off.

Understandably so, of course—the meaning of *like* suggests that people are claiming that everything is "like" itself rather than itself. But as we have seen, words' meanings change, and not just because someone invents a portable listening device and gives it a name composed of words that used to be applied to something else (*Walkman*), but because even the language of people stranded in a cave where life never changed would be under constant transformation. *Like* is a word, and so we'd expect it to develop new meanings: the only question, as always, is which one? So is it that young people are strangely overusing the *like* from the dictionary, or might it be that *like* has birthed a child with a different function altogether? When one alternative involves saddling entire generations of people, of an awesome array of circumstances across a vast nation, with a mysteriously potent inferiority complex, the other possibility beckons as worthy of engagement.

In that light, what has happened to *like* is that it has morphed into a modal marker—actually, one that straddles all the FACE functions as a protean indicator of the human mind at work in conversation. There are actually two modal marker *likes*—that is, to be fluent in modern American English is to have subconsciously internalized not one but two instances of grammar involving *like*.

Let's start with *So we're standing there and there were like grandparents and like grandkids and aunts and uncles all over the place.* That sentence, upon examination, is more than just what the words mean in isolation plus a bizarre squirt of slouchy little *likes*. *Like grandparents and like grandkids* means, when we break down what this teenager was actually trying to communicate, that given the circumstances, you might think it strange that an entire family popped up in this space we expected to be empty for our use, but in fact, it really was a whole family. In that, we have, for one, factuality—"no, really, I mean a family." The original meaning of *like* applies in that one is saying "You may think I mean something *like* a couple and their son, but I mean something *like* a whole brood."

And in that, note that there is also at the same time an acknowledgment of counterexpectation. The new *like* acknowledges unspoken objection while underlining one's own point (the factuality). *Like grandparents* translates here as "There were, despite what you might think, actually grandparents." Another example: *I opened the door and it was, like, her!* certainly doesn't mean "Duhhhh, I suppose it's okay for me to identify the person as her . . ." Vagueness is hardly the issue here. That sentence is uttered to mean "As we all know, I would have expected her father, the next-door neighbor, or some other person, or maybe a phone call or e-mail from her, but instead it was, actually, her." Factuality and counterexpectation in one package, again. It may seem that I am freighting the little word with a bit much, but consider: *It was, like, her!* That sentence has a very precise meaning, despite the fact that because of its socio-logical associations with the young, to many it carries a whiff of Bubble Yum, peanut butter, or marijuana.

We could call that version of *like* "reinforcing *like*." Then there is a second new *like*, which is closer to what people tend to think of all its new uses: it is indeed a hedge. How-ever, that alone doesn't do it justice: we miss that the hedge is just plain nice, something that has further implications for how we place this *like* in a linguistic sense. *This is, like, the only way to make it work* does not mean "Duhhhh, I guess this seems like the way to make it work." A person says this in a context in which the news is unwelcome to the hearer, and this was either mentioned before or, just as likely, is unstatedly obvious. The *like* acknowledges—imagine even a little curtsey—the discomfort. It softens the blow—that is, eases—by swathing the statement in the garb of hypotheti-cality that the basic meaning of *like* lends. Something "like" x is less threatening than x itself; to phrase things as if x were only "like," x is thus like offering a glass of water, a compress, or a warm little blanket. An equivalent is "Let's take our pill now," said by someone who is not, themselves, about to take the pill along with the poor sick person. The sick one knows it, too, but the phrasing with "we" is a soothing fiction, acknowledging that taking pills can be a bit of a drag.

Note that while this new *like* cushions a blow, the blow does get delivered. Rather than being a weak gesture, the new *like* can be seen as gentle but firm. The main point is that it is part of the linguistic system, not something merely littering it up. It isn't surprising that a word meaning "similar to" morphs into a word that quietly allows us to avoid being bumptious, via courteously addressing its likeness rather than the thing itself, via considering it rather than addressing it. Just as uptalk sounds like a question but isn't, *like* sounds like a mere shirk of certainty but isn't, which is why I am avoiding typical terms like "hedging *like*" and "approximative *like*." Those descriptions undershoot what this second usage of *like* is doing: my term will be "easing *like*."

Like *LOL*, *like*, entrenched in all kinds of sentences, used subconsciously, and difficult to parse the real meaning of without careful consideration, has all the hallmarks of a piece of grammar—specifically, in the pragmatic department, modal wing. One thing making it especially clear that the new *like* is not just a tic of heedless, underconfident youth is that many of the people who started using it in the new way in the 1970s are now middle-aged. People's sense of how they talk tends to differ from the reality, and the person of a certain age who claims never to use *like* "that way" as often as not, like, does—and often. As I write, a sentence such as *There were like grandparents and like grandkids in there* is as likely to be spoken by a forty-something as by a teenager or a college student. Just listen around the next time you're standing in a line, watching a talk show, or possibly even listening to yourself.

Then, the two *like*s I have mentioned must be distinguished from yet a third usage, the quotative *like*—as in "And she was like, 'I didn't even invite him.' " This is yet another way that *like* has become grammar. The meaning "similar to" is as natural a source here as it was for *-ly*: mimicking people's utterances is talking similarly to, as in "like," them. Few of the *like*-haters distinguish this *like* from the other new usages, since all are associated with young people and verbal slackerdom. But the third new *like* doesn't do the jobs the others do: there is nothing hesitational or even polite about quotative *like*, much less especially forceful à la the reinforcing *like*. It is a thoroughly straightforward way of quoting a person, often followed by a verbatim mimicry complete with gestures. That's worlds away from *This is, like, the only way to make it work* or *There were like grandkids in there*. Thus the modern American English speaker has mastered not just two, but actually *three* different new usages of *like*.

This third *like*, then, is what linguists call a quotative marker, and that is a piece of grammar, with a job quite similar to the one performed by *that* in a sentence like *He said that it would be okay*. The *that* in this sentence is not a "that" that involves pointing; it's a little tool that links *He said* and *it would be okay*. *He was like, "It's okay"* has the same meaning, expressed with a different grammatical construction.

"Quotative marker" is not a term created just to bend over backward for little *like*. Lots of languages have small words that you insert just before or just after you mention something someone else said. Sometimes they start as a word meaning *that*, sometimes one meaning *say*, or even *do*. It might seem that *like* is somehow a stretch as a source for such a marker, but in fact, in Xhosa, the native language of Nelson Mandela, none other than *like* is used even in formal language. *Ithi* means "like this." *Bible* is iBhayibhile. (See *Bible* tucked into that busy-looking word?) Now, armed with that, look at how you say in Xhosa *The Bible says, "Love thy neighbor"*:

Ithi iBhayibhile "Mthande ummelwane wakho."

You can guess that the words in quotation marks mean "Love thy neighbor." That leaves *Ithi iBhayibhile*, which means "The Bible is like this." In Xhosa, *The Bible says, "Love thy neighbor,"* is "The Bible is like, 'Love thy neighbor' "!

Is There Really No Room for Standards?

For a linguist to hope that the public will give up the idea that some ways of speaking are more appropriate for formal settings than others would be futile—especially since all linguists agree with the public on this. Often we are asked, "If all these things considered bad grammar are really okay, then why don't you use them in your writing and speeches?" However, none of us is pretending that a society of human beings could function in which all spoke or wrote however they wanted to and yet had equal chances at success in life. The linguist's point is that there are no scientific grounds for considering any way of speaking erroneous in some structural or logical sense. To understand this is not to give up on learning to communicate appropriately to context. To understand this is, rather, to shed the contempt: the acrid disgust so many seem to harbor for people who use the forms we have been taught are "bad."

Like is useful here once more. Young people do use it an awful lot, with one in almost every sentence for some stretches. Should they be taught to swallow the *like*s for public speaking or other settings where they want to be taken seriously? Yes! We cannot change that, in real life, whatever the linguist's observations about language change, Shakespeare, *The Great Gatsby*, and DES-pi-kuh-bull, the new *like* will always have a tentative smell about it, even by the time it's been around too long to be called new. The original meaning of *like* as "similar to" coexists as a comparison, and is also easily understood, unlike the baroque subtleties of the new *like*s.

However, those subtleties are real, and cast in a new light the use of the new *like*s in casual speech. It's one thing to agree that young people should be taught to suppress the *like*s in interviews, but harder to not spontaneously go further and hope they stop using the new *like*s completely. After all, if they go part of the way, why not make them finish the job? But a linguist encountering just such a word in an unknown language spoken by a small group in New Guinea, the African rain forest, or the Asian steppes would write fascinated papers on such a multifarious piece of language, with no reason at all to dismiss it as somehow "slangy" or used "too much."

I think of Mualang, a language spoken in Borneo, handy here because it is utterly unknown beyond where it is spoken, and pretty much no one reading this will ever meet a speaker of it. It's just one of the world's thousands of languages, like most of them deeply obscure and almost never committed to paper. It is spoken, only. And all over it is a little word: *tih*. This *tih* can pop up several times in the same sentence. It's hard to quite nail what *tih* "means"—something about calling attention to something, making sure the person you're talking to is following your point. It all sounds a lot like *you know* or, yes, one of the new *like*s. If someone had occasion to spend time with the speakers of Mualang, if they learned the language, one indication of their true fluency would be their peppering their speech with *tih*, which would make this person's Mualang "real." I doubt any of us would venture to say that there was just too much *tih* in Mualang, any more than we would claim that there was too much or too little of anything in it. If confronted with Mualang, we would take it on its own terms, as being what it is. There is no historical documentation of a language like Mualang, but we can be quite sure that *tih* arose from a morphing, in the past, of some other word that had a different meaning. Yet on what grounds, we would wonder, could anyone say that anything in Mualang was "wrong"?

There is no reason we cannot view our own English that way in terms of casual speech. English's new *like*s are like *tih*s. We can treat spraying for *like*s in public speaking as a matter of fashion that one must knuckle under to. After all, one simply *cannot* wear a crinoline to a job interview, and nudity would be awkward at most dinner parties. However, we can also understand that casual speech full of *like*s is not, in truth, tentative or messy, but empathic and polite.

Some might have preferred, or even expected, that in a book about how language changes, the issue of standards would have been the focus throughout. However, in my view, the spectacle of how language changes is more interesting, and more useful to the collective intelligence of a civilization, than the issue as to whether we should regret the changes. In fact, the content of this book makes it rather clear that any such regret would seem to qualify as subjective, local, a matter of preference that a broader perspective sheds a different light on.

One often cannot truly know what it is to be an American until one has spent time somewhere else. The idea that any new development in a language could be "bad" feels as authoritative as one's sense of up and down—until one sees that the exact same things thrive in other languages where sensible people never even notice them. We might also consider that the fury some harbor over language usage issues is incommensurate with the gravity of the issue. Does anyone genuinely fear that we are on our way to babbling incomprehensibly to one another when no such thing has ever happened among a single human group in the history of our species? One suspects more afoot than logic: rage over language usage may be the last permissible open classism, channeling a tribalist impulse roiling ever underneath.

The tribalist impulse has ever fewer officialized outlets

in our society, in which open discrimination is increasingly barred from the public forum. The very pointedness of the rage behind so many comments about language usage suggests something exploding after a considerable buildup of pressure, denied regular venting. In this grand and tragic world of ours, it is rather unexpected, in itself, that anyone would experience anger in response to the construction of a sentence. *A student can hand in* their *paper anytime after Thursday*—this use of *their* is grounds for fulmination amid global warming, terrorism, grisly epidemics, and the prospect of a world without bees?

Nevertheless, language standards will always be with us to some extent. I hope a sense of language change as a parade can coax us to think of the standards as a matter not of logic but of fashion. One must at least pay lip service to fashion, but no one thinks the fact that we no longer use attachable collars is a moral issue. There are times you have to tuck in your shirt (or, as it were, your *like*s), but no one sees a person with his shirttail out at home as a blackguard.*

Meanwhile, the show goes on. Changes are always happening, sometimes detected and reviled, sometimes creeping in unnoticed. The quotative *like* isn't the only new quotative marker: *all* is used in the same way, as in *And he was all "You better watch out."* There was a time when someone followed this *all* with an actual imitation of the person. However, for a while now, people have been using this *all* expression in an increasingly matter-of-fact way: *And he was*

---

* Which is pronounced "blaggerd," which makes it a new word from two in everything but the spelling, like *daisy* and *breakfast*.

all "So when's the party?" and I was all "Just ask me tomorrow when I have it all organized," and he was all "But I need to know now," and I'm all . . . One now hears young people using *all* in this way without intending any particular drama. In other words, *all* is becoming a piece of grammar, just one more bit of stuff that doesn't "mean" anything but gets a job done.

Interesting: if our brains weren't on writing, and English were an unwritten language that people just talked, with little concern as to whether it was changing from century to century, then *all* would possibly be the beginning of a new verb. It might work like this: *I'm all*, said endlessly across generations, could start to be heard as "I maw," with the final *l* sound on *all* softening and falling away. If this also happened with *you're all* and *he/she's all*, then we would have this process:

TODAY	SOMEDAY
I'm all	I maw
You're all	you raw
He's all	he zaw

The fun thing would be that this would be a highly irregular verb. There are times when an English speaker might almost have Irregularity Envy toward other languages. Native speakers of French or Russian effortlessly manage verbs that take a menagerie of different forms depending on person, number, and tense, but in English the only real contender we have to this is *to be* and its wild mashup of *am, is, been, were*, etc. Imagine if we also had a new verb that meant *say*, where one had to memorize *I maw, you raw*, but *she zaw*, and we could listen to learners messing it up and saying, "I zaw."

Certainly, though, we have a new grammar word from *all*, whose meaning no one could have predicted would come to be "say," any more than anyone could know that a word for "body" could come to be an adverbial suffix.

Meanwhile, *no* has become a word that by all rights should arouse the same animus that *literally* does: it is used as often to mean its opposite as to mean what we think of it as meaning. To wit, think of a modern American exchange like this:

DIANA: They kept saying nobody would get there on time, and everybody ended up there ahead of schedule.

FRANCESCA: No, the trains are actually running properly now, it's amazing.

Why "no" when the person is agreeing? Taken literally, a "no" like this could be read as oddly confrontational; yet today it is an established part of casual American conversation. I myself participated in an exchange in which I said, "And so you wound up loving it here in Toledo," and the other person said, "No, we have a five-bedroom house and a garden!" Again, that exchange makes no sense if we insist, as a dictionary would, that *no* negates.

Things are changing. This usage of *no* does make sense on the basis of what *no* "should" mean, actually. Francesca's "no" is negating something implied: other people's denial of Diana's take on the matter, with which Francesca agrees. Francesca is saying "no" to the people who thought nobody would get there on time, therefore agreeing with Diana's line of reasoning, which is to argue that the trains are better than they used to be. The person I was talking to was denying the implied others who would perhaps not expect that someone would be excited about moving to Toledo, as opposed to, say, San Francisco.

However, to the extent that we are not accustomed to thinking of implied contradiction as part of what a word "means," this new *no* can seem odd, just as *totally*, with its similar function of refuting implied naysayers, can seem overused. Both are just how language keeps going, as each generation comes up with slightly off interpretations of what they hear from the previous one.

And so the forms and meanings of words sail along. One that I have experienced, as someone rounding fifty as this book goes to press, is *based off of. My point is based off of what Lily said*, my students will say, and I blink a couple of times, internally at least, since my sense is that the term is *based on*. However, there is nothing inherently better about *based on*—*based off of* conveys movement from the base and could therefore be considered more vivid. Really, it's a six versus half dozen kind of difference, with *based off of* having randomly caught on of late. The reason its proliferation has struck me is that it indeed took off especially in the 1990s, after I was already an adult. Make no mistake, language change can throw me a bit, too. *Based off of* first struck me as a tad clunky, I must admit, for reasons that are quite arbitrary.* However, in light of *awesome* and *awful*, *hey* and *huh*, *reduce* meaning "go back to" versus "go down to," *merry* having once meant "short," and so much else, there is no basis upon which I could present anything called judgment. *Based off of* is just one more symptom of the fact that the language a people speak is properly *the stage a language is in as they are speaking it*.

All these novelties can't help but seem like just that, novelties, with the air of triviality and impermanance associated with that word. However, a new view of language requires hearing things like this as the essence of what language is, rather than as interruptions of a stasis that has, in fact, never existed. One must avoid being, for example, Jonathan Swift.

Yes, we'd all like to have written *Gulliver's Travels* and "A Modest Proposal." However, Swift was also a highly language-conscious person who heard English's moving on as a desecration. Let's listen in on him in 1712, complaining about people "abbreviating words." He finds the abbreviations in question to be "such harsh unharmonious sounds that none but a northern ear could endure," the idea in his time being that the dialects of northern England were less quaint than irritating. But what "abbreviation" was bothering Mr. Swift? Why, the *-ed* past suffix *pronounced as it is now*. He was used to it always being pronounced as we

---

* Linguists have biases indeed. One expression I just "don't like"—although I "patch" myself into accepting it as another example of form and meaning splitting harmlessly apart as with uptalk—is *Can I get a . . . ?* when ordering food. The *get* sounds, just, *coarse* to me. And yet everybody says it. I'm used to it now. Really, I am . . .

today pronounce *blessed* as "bless-id" in religious contexts. Swift couldn't handle hearing the excrescence all around him of pronunciations like "drudg'd, disturb'd, rebuk'd, fledg'd, and a thousand others everywhere to be met . . . we form so jarring a sound, and so difficult to utter, that I have often wondered how it ever could obtain."

"But you're shortening the word! You spell *rebuked* with an *e* before the *d*—why don't you pronounce it?" Swift would ask us. Quite easily we would dismiss him with "Get over it—it chang'd." If anything, we wish he could have viewed the shortening of -*ed* as English becoming the form of itself we are so cozy with today, since to us, our own stage of the language seems so right, so inevitable, where we can say "kist" rather than "kiss-id" without a man in stockings rapping us on the knuckles. But we, too, are present at just a stage in the language. In our discomfort with signs that new stages are coming as they always have, we become Swifts.

We don't need to. "Variety is the spice of life," we say. We may wonder what the new fashions will be. We admire the old person who keeps trying new things. We behold the history of Western music with awe, dazzled by the endless transformations over time. The term *move on* strikes us in a good place; *stay put*, not so much. The lava lamp mesmerizes; the apple cut in half turning brown does not. Yet, somehow, language is supposed to be different.

Language must stay put because novelty is ugly? Ugly as in words like *kissed*, *rolled*, and *believed*? It must stay put because if it doesn't we won't understand one another? But that never happened as English went from being an alternate-universe German to what it is now; language change is communal, not idiosyncratic. It must stay put because . . . we want the story to just stop cold? We don't want to know how it comes out? We don't want it to come out at all? Little Red Riding Hood knocked on the door. And knocked. And knocked again. Then, she knocked. Again. Little Red Riding Hood knocked, as always, on the door, upon which she then knocked on the door. She's knocking now. She will knock on the door afterward, and continue to do so. Knock knock. Knock.

The Victorians had a practice of grouping elaborately costumed people into poses inspired by paintings to make what was called a "tableau vivant." The tableau would be part of a social event, with ladies grinning as they stood frozen, striking their painterly poses. "How charming! How lovely!" people would say.

But today the practice seems as bizarre as feeding people to lions. It made more sense before film and color print reproduction, and it was also often used as an excuse to ogle women scantily clad. Yet, from our vantage point, it still seems odd that anyone would watch people striking a pose when you could watch them performing a play. Or even just walking down the street, as long as they moved!

This tableau tradition is analogous to the dictionary. The language poses sweetly between its covers, caught one afternoon and made to hold still. The dictionary is handy in ways just as the tableaux were—but it does not represent what a language is any more than the tableau represented actual existence. Let's enjoy not a snapshot of the language, but its living reality: as a show, a process, a parade. Let's watch it going by, wondering what's next. Or even, let's join it. The language lives, as we do. Let's love it as what it is—something always becoming, never still.

Maybe some prefer their flowers pressed dry in books. There are those with affectionate feelings toward the inflatable doll and the corpse. Surely, though, most of us seek life. Language, too, lives. We must take a deep breath and, like the people initially so put off by Darwinism, embrace reality, this time linguistic. Among the many benefits of doing so: wonder replaces disgust, curiosity replaces condemnation, and overall, you have a lot more fun.

Notes

1. THE FACES OF ENGLISH

15 Linguists adopted the term *pragmatism*: Those either familiar with this territory or interested in investigating it further should recall or learn, respectively, that amid the relevant scholarship, which straddles conventionalized academic sub-areas and is prolific to a degree that works against consensus, terminology is often fuzzy and the canonical concept is elusive. Analysts differ on where semantics leaves off and pragmatics begins. Also, unlike conventional lists of prepositions or conjunctions, there is no agreement as to which pragmatic words are dedicated to indicating personal involvement (modal pragmatic markers) as opposed to other aspects of pragmatics such as emphasis and starting new topics, etc. My FACE conglomeration corresponds mainly to what M. A. K. Halliday classified as the "interpersonal mode" of language in his classic "Language Structure and Language Function," in *New Horizons*

in Linguistics, ed. by John Lyons (Harmondsworth: Penguin, 1970).

The FACE items are often discussed under the heading of "discourse particle," but that refers to pragmatics in general rather than the attitudinal wing. "Modal particle" gets around, primarily in reference to German, but sometimes by extension to other languages. However, many of the words in question are too big to be called particles; "particle" is not really a grammatical category; and often it's more than one word (or even things like intonation) that does the same job as modal "particles." Plus, modality can be semantic as well as pragmatic, encompassing, for example, people's assessment of probability, as in *That must be the Indian food*. Probability is more semantic in having meaning in the conventional sense: it is not an optional "add-on" to a sentence in the way that saying *well*, . . . is.

Hence, FACE.

16 what linguists call modal pragmatic markers: My favorite source is the academic but thoroughly readable monograph *Grammaticalization and Discourse Functions*, by Laurel Brinton (Berlin: Mouton de Gruyter, 1996).

16 words of all kinds are always going personal: Useful discussion is in Elizabeth Traugott and Richard Dasher's *Regularity in Semantic Change* (Cambridge: Cambridge University Press, 2005).

22 in one language called Seko Padang: Thomas E. Payne, *Describing Morphosyntax* (Cambridge: Cambridge University Press, 1997), p. 255.

27 "Written words are isolated from the fuller context": Walter J. Ong, *Orality and Literacy* (London: Routledge, 1982), p. 101.

34 "pretense of shared knowledge that achieves intimacy": Brinton, *Grammaticalization and Discourse Functions*, p. 186. For a whole book on *you know* (yes, there is such a thing!), try Jan-Ola Östman, *"You Know": A Discourse Functional View* (Amsterdam: John Benjamins, 1981).

34 *Hwæt! We gardena in geardagum*: Brinton, *Grammaticalization and Discourse Functions*, pp. 181–210.

38   In English, profanity plays its role here: *The Random House Dictionary of American Slang*, Vol. 1, ed. by J. E. Lighter (New York: Random House, 1994), pp. 44–45.

41   Or, in a language of Nepal called Kham: David E. Watters, "Kham," in *The Sino-Tibetan Languages*, ed. by Graham Thurgood and Randy J. LaPolla (London: Routledge, 2003), p. 703.

41   The sheer amount of laughter in typical conversation: Handy are articles in *The Psychology of Humor: An Integrative Approach*, ed. by Rod A. Martin (Burlington, VT: Elsevier Academic, 2007). A key academic article is Matthew Gervais and David Sloan Wilson, "The Evolution and Functions of Laughter and Humor: A Synthetic Approach," *The Quarterly Review of Biology* 80 (2005): 395–430.

42   the nature of texting's abbreviation LOL: Katie Heaney, "The Twelve Meanings of LOL," Buzzfeed.com, http://www.buzz feed.com/katieheaney/the-12-meanings-of-lol.

49   language evolution theorist Michael Tomasello: The book to consult is Michael Tomasello, *Origins of Human Communication* (Cambridge, MA: MIT Press, 2008).

50   easing is central to classic descriptions of how politeness works: Especially well-known is Roger Brown and Albert Gilman, "The Pronouns of Power and Solidarity," *Language and Social Context*, ed. by Pier Paolo Giglioli (London: Penguin, 1972), pp. 252–82. (This article was also reprinted in other anthologies.) Less easily available but equally useful is Robin Lakoff, "What You Can Do with Words: Politeness, Pragmatics and Performatives," in *Proceedings of the Texas Conference on Performatives, Presuppositions, and Implicatures*, ed. by Andy Rogers, Bob Wall, and John Murphy (Arlington, VA: Center for Applied Linguistics, 1977), pp. 79–106.

53   often they will slide into using some signs with their speech: I learned of this from professional signer Alek Lev, to whom I am sincerely grateful for the information, especially given in such detail.

2. IT'S THE IMPLICATION THAT MATTERS

In this chapter, unless otherwise specified, word histories are based on entries in *The Oxford English Dictionary*.

67   "'Credit' has been reversified": John Lanchester, "Money Talks," *New Yorker*, August 14, 2014.

85   Shakespeare is, again, a useful demonstration: Mark H. Liddell, "Botching Shakespeare," *Atlantic Monthly*, October 1898. My most summary presentation of the argument was a hundred years later, in my *The Word on the Street: Debunking the Myth of a "Pure" Standard English* (New York: Plenum, 1998), namely chap. 4. For an intelligent objection (followed, of course, by a response from me!), find "Translating Shakespeare into English: A Debate," *Voice and Speech Review* 7 (2011): 38–51, where David Crystal and Ben Crystal weigh in from the other side.

3. WHEN WORDS STOP BEING WORDS

102   Sylvester and Tweety cartoon: "Home Tweet Home," 1950.

104   Carl's Jr. restaurant receipt: From the blog *Excessive Exclamation*.

104   Old issues of *Archie*: *Archie's Pals and Gals* 127, October 1978. Somehow Love Canal never made it into the stories; nor was the Carter presidency ever referred to. No, I *didn't* have all that much better to do: you'll glean that I barely dated as a teen. For example, the girl who hauled us out of *Body Heat* soonish thereafter proceeded to have experiences that likely rendered her less likely to find scenes like the one in that movie so shocking, while I was still stuck with *Archie* and *Peanuts*.

108   a brand-new language, called a creole: Okay, creole language specialists—a very few may note that a creole called Palenquero, spoken in a small community of descendants of escaped slaves in Colombia, with Spanish words, has a prefix, *ma-*, to express the plural. But that's because all the slaves in question

spoke the same language (Kikongo) in which that prefix happened to be the plural marker. Most creole languages were created by slaves speaking several languages, in which there was no way that any trait from one language would make it into the language being created. Hence the way creole languages usually indicate the plural is with a *word* taken from the colonizer language, given that all that the slaves knew of the language for the most part was words, rather than any prefix or suffix from a language any of the slaves spoke natively.

123 "A noble spirit embiggens the smallest man": "Lisa the Iconoclast," *The Simpsons*, Fox, 1996.

123 The Old English verbal ending . . . Latin lost its noun case: I describe this process in my book *What Language Is* (New York: Gotham, 2011), or for those up for detail so mind-numbing I suspect exactly two human beings have ever read it, my book *Language Interrupted: Signs of Non-Native Acquisition in Standard Language Grammars* (New York: Oxford University Press, 2007).

124 "We saw *Wes' Side Story*" . . . "I kiss' my daughter": What determines whether something gets elided or not is a topic that requires statistical analysis to engage productively, but this means that the literature on it cannot qualify as pleasure reading. However, an article I have always found to cover the matter artfully nevertheless, because of the lapidary writing and basic lucidity of its author, is Gregory Guy, "Explanation in Variable Phonology: An Exponential Model of Morphological Constraints," *Language Variation and Change* 3 (1991): 1–22.

126 Latin changed when imposed upon subjects of the spreading Roman Empire: This analysis of the birth of the Romance languages is less conventionally aired than the one about English, but is in my view obviously accurate, or at least obviously enough to be appropriately broadcast here. The arguments are not in user-friendly places, but for those interested, try R. De Dardel and J. Wüest, "Les systèmes casuels du proto-Roman: Les deux cycles de simplification," *Vox Romanica* 52 (1993): 25–65; or if just by chance you'd rather read in English, Stéphane

Goyette, "From Latin to Early Romance: A Case of Partial Creolization?" *Language Change and Language Contact in Pidgins and Creoles*, ed. by me (Amsterdam: John Benjamins, 2000), pp. 103–31.

132 Australian Dyirbal, in which there were four classes: Those groupings cannot help but stir wonder, and for more of the story (what goes into the classes is based as much on how words sound as what they mean), a great source is Keith Plaster and Maria Polinsky, "Women Are Not Dangerous Things: Gender and Categorization," *Harvard Working Papers in Linguistics* 12 (Cambridge, MA: Harvard University Department of Linguistics, 2007).

4. A VOWEL IS A PROCESS

136 *betch*, a transformation of the word *bitch*: Katie J. M. Baker, "Beyond 'Jappy': It's All About the Betches Now," *Jezebel*, June 28, 2013.

144 International Phonetic Alphabet: Here are the symbols for these sounds, from which many will understand why I refrain from using them in the text—this book isn't supposed to be school.

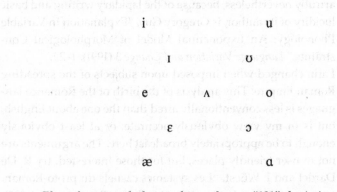

Plus, these symbols are themselves a "101" depiction. Those already schooled in the International Phonetic Alphabet (IPA)

will miss the schwa (ə), similar to the *uh* sound but slightly higher, a little smudge of a sound we use in unaccented syllables such as the *-on* of *lemon* and the *a-* of *about*. Others will know that when we say *boat*, most of us are not using the straight "o" sound in this chart, which technically stands for a pure "oh" that someone speaking Spanish would use. Really, the sound is the "o" plus a tail of "oo," written as *ow* in the IPA. "Boh-oot," we say, just as we say "bay-eet" for *bait* (in IPA, *ej*). To actually say *bait* without the tail of ee-ness is to sound like the working-class people on *Downton Abbey* when they say "Mr. Bates," just as to pronounce *boat* with no tail of oo-ness is to sound like Minnesotans. These things get multifarious; better, for our purposes, to stick with *beet* and *bait*, which give us a good start. If it leaves you wanting to know more about this "code" called the International Phonetic Alphabet, there are endless online sources, complete with audio samples.

149   Northern Cities Shift: I am presenting only a part of the entire phenomenon: the "train" is longer. The process is comprehensively described in William Labov, Sharon Ash, and Charles Boberg, *The Atlas of North American English* (Berlin: De Gruyter Mouton, 2006), one of an imposing number of seminal works by Labov, who is largely responsible for spearheading the identification and documentation of sound changes such as these in America. The volume in question is not designed for leisure reading, however. To get just a sense of how these shifted vowels actually sound, check online for an interview with Labov himself on the subject.

160   there is also a vowel shift happening in California: This has been brought to attention by Penelope Eckert, for example, in "Where Do Ethnolects Stop?" *International Journal of Bilingualism* 12 (2008) 25–42. As with the Northern Cities Shift, I am describing the process only to an introductory degree. The full web of shifts would wear out all but a few dozen academic readers—but would also only underline the extent to which vowels are like the bees a hive is crawling with.

161 *The Many Loves of Dobie Gillis*: "Taken to the Cleaners," CBS, 1960.

170 "The now fashionable pronunciation": Morchard Bishop, ed., *Recollections of the Table-Talk of Samuel Rogers* (London: Richards, 1952), cited in David Crystal, *The Stories of English* (New York: Overlook Press, 2004).

5. LEXICAL SPRINGTIME

174 *The Lucy Show*: "Lucy Gets Her Maid," CBS, 1964.

175 perfectly humble words that combine a pair of meanings: For a history of today's contractions, see Barren Brainerd, "The Contractions of *Not*: A Historical Note," *Journal of English Linguistics* 22 (1989): 176–96.

185 *The Mary Tyler Moore Show*: "The Courtship of Mary's Father's Daughter," CBS, 1973.

187 *The Dick Van Dyke Show*: "The Return of Edwin Karp," CBS, 1964.

187 the Backshift exhibits some irregularities: An article on the subject suggesting a cocktail of factors responsible is Ingo Plag, Gero Kunter, Sabine Lappe, and Maria Braun, "The Role of Semantics, Argument Structure, and Lexicalization in Compound Stress Assignment in English," *Language* 84 (2008): 760–94. What strikes me about this article other than its interesting content is that the authors are all German and yet command English well enough to know how Anglophones accent their compound words. I am alternately envious of, amazed by, and sympathetic to scholars born to languages other than English who actually have to perform academically, including live, at conferences, in English, a language not native to them.

193 *Road* in Old English: I base this on a discussion by Anatoly Liberman in his blog on Oxford University Press's website, August 20, 2014, http://blog.oup.com/2014/08/road-word-origin-etymology/.

194 how some people pronounce *nuclear* as "nucular": A degree of guesswork has surrounded this pronunciation, but some

entries in *Language Log* seem to have nailed the issue, and I have based my explanation on them. Especially useful are ones by Geoff Nunberg, October 5, 2008, and Steven Pinker, October 17, 2008.

6. THIS IS YOUR BRAIN ON WRITING

209   "It's been proved" . . . *shat* as the past of *shit*: The handiest way to see these changes in our times is with Google's Ngram viewer, which shows the usage of words and combinations of words in print over the centuries.

211   *like*: Alexanda D'Arcy, "*Like* and Language Ideology: Disentangling Fact from Fiction," *American Speech* 82 (2007): 386–419. This article is so readable that I highly recommend it even to laymen. However, she defines not just three but four *likes*. In my presentation, "easing" *like* corresponds to what she calls an "approximative adverb," while what she classifies as separate "discourse marker" and "discourse particle" *likes* are what I am calling "reinforcing *like*." In my view, these "discourse" usages have a more definite function than D'Arcy dwells upon, and essentially a single one rather than two.

220   in Xhosa . . . *Ithi* means "like this": Herbert W. Pahl, A. M. Pienaar, and T. A. Ndungane, eds., *The Greater Dictionary of Xhosa* (Alice, South Africa: University of Fort Hare, 1989).

222   Mualang: Johnny Tjia, *A Grammar of Mualang: An Ibanic Language of Western Kalimantan, Indonesia* (Utrecht: LOT, 2007).

228   Swift: "A Proposal for Correcting, Improving, and Ascertaining the English Tongue, in a Letter to the Most Honourable Robert Earl of Oxford and Mortimer, Lord High Treasurer of Great Britain," printed 1712. In the letter, Swift's complaint is aimed specifically at the use of the shortened -*ed* form in poetry and prose, rather than speech. However, his meaning makes it clear that he would consider the use of the "shortened" form in speech as equally barbarous, as he can barely even imagine wrapping his lips around it.

Acknowledgments

For this book, my greatest thanks go to the undergraduates at Columbia University who have taken courses from me on language and linguistics. It is through these endlessly brilliant people that I have gained a sense over the past several years of what interests people about language and why, something quite different from what tends to interest linguists themselves.

It's easy for an academic to quietly dismiss what laymen tend to ask as "beside the point," not what we really study, best dispensed with as quickly (albeit politely) as possible in the hope of getting across at least a little of the "real" stuff. However, I have increasingly found that these questions from the outside often stimulate thoroughly interesting investigations. It gradually occurred to me that my students' questions and observations, as well as those from e-mail correspondents and callers-in to talk shows, centered mostly on matters that would be usefully covered in single presentation.

The heart of the matter (ever confusing, ever fascinating) is the difference between print and speech, vaster than it seems. Print is a statue, speech is the person; print is a drawing, speech is the thing; print is a snapshot, speech is the life—and yet, gracious, it's hard to truly feel that from day to day. My students have, with intelligence and wit, spurred me on in seeking to help the public see language plain.

I also owe endless thanks to Paul Golob for lending me the experience of having a book of mine edited in an attentive fashion I haven't experienced since the days of Napster, Yellowtail wine as the new big thing, and kale still over the horizon. To have someone serve as a rigorous intermediary between me and the curious layman I consider myself to write for has been refreshing, welcome, and necessary. Thanks also to Harold Itzkowitz for finding me some dandy examples of pre-Backshift examples from early television and ancient movies.

Thanks also to Katinka Matson for believing in me after all these years (I have now known her so long that the day I met her was the day I encountered my first *digital camera!*), and to the people who disagree with me about Shakespeare for—although I doubt this was their mission—stimulating me to continue pushing my point.

Index